THE I.T. GUY

Real life IT support in dangerous locations

Graeme Simpson

theitguy@simmo.gs

To my Grandad Jack

who honed my sense
of adventure and taught
me a perseverance
I never knew I had.

PART ONE

INTRODUCTION AND BACKGROUND

CHAPTER ONE

Introduction

This is not an autobiography, but an autobiographical account of my travels. My intention is for the focus to be on the travels, rather than me.

For a period in my life, I happened to find myself in particularly unusual and interesting situations. I'm not a soldier, a warrior or a hero but I'm hoping my ordinariness will make my tales more relatable. They may even be aspirational.

Given that I am the author, what follows is naturally my opinion, how I saw and experienced the events. Mistakes will have crept in over time due to poor recollection or simply the natural inclination towards a rose-tinted view of the past.

For the purposes of privacy, I have stuck to using first names only throughout. I have even changed a few of them, sometimes to maintain a person's privacy and dignity, and sometimes because I genuinely can't remember their name.

In one or two rare places, I've simplified events or situations slightly for the purpose of brevity or clarity. You'll have to trust me; the tale is better for it.

I hope you enjoy reading this book, my first foray into the

world of publishing. I've certainly enjoyed writing it.

I would like to thank my wife Sophy for all her hard work in bringing this book to fruition. Thanks to you're hard work, their is less mitsakes now than there wood have bean.

Thank you also to the various friends and relatives that took the time to read this in various states of draft-yness.

CHAPTER TWO

Background

"Looks like we need to call the IT guy" is said many thousands of times a day across the land. Working in IT can be like being in the emergency services. Not nearly as important as the Police, Fire or Ambulance obviously, and likely not even in the top ten after such noble teams as lifeboat crews or mountain rescue. I'm guessing most people would rate car breakdown services higher than IT support. But there are those occasions when a less urgent problem arises and no one else other than the IT guy[1] can help.

However, from the way you can be called in to sort it out, you might think the building was burning down. If you're working on the frontline of IT support, you need to get used to working under pressure. You have to give an air of calm confidence while a nervous customer paces around behind you, butting in frequently to ask how things are going.

As well as sorting out the problem with the required calm

---

[1] I would just like to acknowledge here that although there are many capable and highly skilled women working in IT, it remains a sector heavily dominated by men.

demeanour, you're also thinking how to explain a potentially very technical problem to someone who's always on the cusp of not really grasping it. But then again, sometimes you just reboot their machine.

Clearly, I'm not saving anyone's life in these situations – but sometimes I would be saving an aspect of someone's life. It could be weeks of work, financial information or even years of family photos. And at the risk of blowing my own trumpet, I think I have been pretty good at being the IT guy.

As well as keeping a relatively calm head under pressure, I could probably be considered fairly adventurous. I would like to give you an example of my adventurous spirit from my childhood, one of those classics that I or any of my family members might roll out with equal enthusiasm. It ably demonstrates a casual attitude to rules, a small degree of crazy coupled with sensible planning.

Aged around twelve, I went to France on an exchange with a family we already knew. Because it was outside of a regular school arrangement, I travelled solo by plane rather than the usual trial-by-coach. Amongst other aspects of French life, I was introduced to the huge fun of banger fireworks, which didn't have the inconvenience of an age restriction on purchase. I bought a couple of hundred of them to take back to the UK with me, strung together in blocks of fifty and each one smaller than my childish little finger.

Even at that age, I knew that smuggling small explosives onto a plane could land me in hot water, but I was still determined to try. I reckoned that I shouldn't put them in the hold or the sniffer dogs might find them. Equally, I knew I couldn't put them in my carry-on bag as they might show up on the x-ray machine. That left only carrying them on my person, so I split the lining of my coat and slipped them inside.

On reflection, boarding an aircraft with explosives

strapped to my chest probably wasn't the wisest choice. Nowadays I'd probably be locked up, regardless of my young age. But I'd clearly thought it out and I was, thankfully, successful in my plan. At no point did I get arrested or accidentally set them off in a series of loud and impromptu bangs. It would have been quite an accomplishment to be added to a terrorist watchlist before reaching my teenage years. Luckily, airline security was a little bit more relaxed in the late 1980s.

I like this story from my childhood. Quite apart from the derring-do, it shows a remarkable level of planning and situational awareness that even now I'm quite impressed with. I think these characteristics held me in good stead later.

Skip forward, and by my mid-twenties I had gained a degree in computer science and was living and working in Hereford. I was running my own business but, owing to a poor choice of business partner, I was looking for an escape. And so my tale starts properly, with the seemingly mundane task of looking for a new job.

PART TWO

LONDON

CHAPTER THREE

The best interview

Having decided to find a new job, I started hunting around for both potential employers and a reference or two. At the time I was loosely friends with a chap called John who was serving in the SAS. For those that don't already know, the SAS, or Special Air Service, is a British elite special forces unit with roots going back to World War 2. It has been based in Hereford since 1960 and the city is rightly (but quietly) proud to host it.

Naturally there are some running jokes, including the idea that in Hereford 'everyone knows a SAS man' which frequently turns out to be true. I really did happen to know an SAS man and I thought John would make an excellent reference for the applications I was expecting to soon be sending out.

I approached John and he happily agreed to my request. But he also responded immediately, saying that he thought he knew someone that might be interested in employing me. Did I fancy going down to London to have a chat with his friend? Well, why not? I had thought that finding another job would be quite long winded, so I was pleased that I'd found a possibility so quickly as well as excited that it was far outside of my expectations.

Weeks or perhaps only days later, John took me down to London for personal introductions. We drove down in a BMW M5 that John had borrowed from a mate, although he drove it like he'd stolen it. We were to meet up with Johnny, co-founder of a company called Olive Security.

At that time, Olive was in its early days but making a reasonable name for itself. Staffed entirely by ex-military personnel, largely from Hereford, they provided niche security services to the rich and paranoid. They were particularly keen to add more technical skills to their portfolio, which is where I came in.

I didn't realise it then, but I'd already got the job before setting off. In that world, a personal recommendation was pretty much sufficient and as Olive was growing, they were glad to have new people on board. My interview with Johnny was therefore a quick check to make sure I wasn't a complete fool and then mostly him presenting to me on why I should join their merry band.

To be fair, I was already pretty sold. The offices were located just off Berkeley Square in Mayfair, London. While the offices themselves weren't exactly glamorous, it was an exciting location, particularly for someone relatively young (25 at the time) and naïve. Opposite the Mayfair office was a private members club, where the Queen Mother could occasionally be seen exiting, slightly the worse for wear after a tipple or two. I wasn't used to having royalty visiting next-door, regardless of their sobriety, so this felt like a new world to me.

After going out for a quick lunch, I was told to go and have a bit of fun in London for the afternoon. I have no idea what I did for the few spare hours, but I duly returned at the end of the working day to meet the rest of the team and to head out for some drinks.

This is where the fun started and it remains my personal 'best interview ever'. We hit some bars in Mayfair and I remember trying to balance keeping up my drinking efforts with the others versus not being completely smashed. As someone that probably slides in comfortably under the average height bar, I'm never going to manage to keep up with a load of ex-squaddies in the drinking stakes. But that didn't mean I wasn't going to try and put in a good effort. I distinctly remember someone asking me if I'd like another beer. I still had the last one in my hand unfinished, so I politely declined. "There you go" came the response to my refusal and I was handed yet another bottle.

Thankfully, at some point the need for more beer was overtaken by the need for food. We headed to an upmarket restaurant in one of the many sub-pavement clubs that surround Mayfair. At this point I was grinning a lot and having a lovely time, but also with that sober version of myself still clinging on in the back of my mind, telling me to hang tight as vomiting wouldn't help my job prospects much.

The waiter came round to take the drinks orders and I tried to discreetly order a soft drink. I was overheard by one of the Olive team who demanded that the waiter 'bring him a proper drink'. Thankfully the waiter realised that a 'proper drink' would likely lead to a 'proper mess' and mouthed "I'll bring you a Coke", before turning smartly on his heels.

It must have been at this time that Harry arrived. Harry was definitely what most people would describe as 'a character'. He arrived loudly, apologising for being a bit late because he'd crashed his moped leaving St James Palace. Harry then stood back looking a bit confused.

"Oh, bloody hell", he declared, "I've got the Admiral's jacket on".

Harry had a bit more Royal blood than the rest of us mere mortals, and even more Royal connections. And apparently, someone else's jacket.

I don't know why particularly, but Harry's arrival seemed the icing on the cake. I was in hook, line and sinker with this team of super soldiers and crazies.

My only regret from that evening is that I have no idea what I ate. It was probably one of the nicest meals I've ever had, but it will be forever lost to me behind the haze of booze and time.

Still, at some point I must have said yes, and agreed to sign up to Team Olive. These guys were fun, lively and not afraid to splash out on a fancy steak dinner (or maybe it was lobster?).

CHAPTER FOUR

The Prince in the Tower

I wasn't the only person joining Olive at that time. Two others from Hereford also started at about the same period, Baz and Mark, both of whom were finishing military careers in 264 SAS Signal Squadron, the Signals regiment attached to the SAS and also based in Hereford. Including Mark, Baz and myself, the company now numbered about a dozen. We three split our time between London and Hereford, whereas everyone else was exclusively London based (even if most of them also actually lived in Hereford, at least at the weekends).

It's worth pointing out that I was the first non ex-military person to be employed by Olive. Apart from a stint in the Scouts, I'd never held rank or worn a beret. Despite this, I never felt the odd one out and my skills driving a keyboard seemed to hold me in reasonable esteem with my colleagues.

There were, however, occasional difficulties with language. Not only do the military have their own language, but it varies depending on which branch. In the Army, a cup of tea is a *brew*, whereas in the Marines it's a *wet*. I had to learn as I went along, and it felt more like I was in the gang when I could understand the secret language.

We had a small office in Hereford but we went to London frequently. The combination of the limited funds of a startup company and what the team were used to, meant that accommodation while in London was a little bit rough. Our offices in Mayfair doubled up as sleeping quarters. Hidden behind a cupboard in each office you could usually find a mattress that would be pulled out in the evening. Other facilities for our luxury accommodation included a shower and a microwave! Despite the posh Mayfair address it felt more like student accommodation. In fact, my student digs had been much better appointed, including, as they did, an actual bed and a real kitchen.

Given that I wasn't permanently based in London, I was much lower in the pecking order for floor sleeping space. I tended to find a spot wherever I could, with the last choice being the windowless bunk room in the basement. It was cramped, airless and apparently everyone else's last choice as well. Apart from treating myself to a mildly luxurious sleeping bag, these arrangements were probably at odds with what most people expected from a job and accommodation based in Mayfair. According to Monopoly at least, it's the best location in London!

If nothing was going on, it tended to be a bit boring. I don't actually remember doing much at all on quiet nights other than watching films on a laptop. Most of the chaps seemed to use the time to hit the gym, which I never bothered with. Thankfully, there were more than enough nights where something was going on, often including going on jobs.

At that time, Olive's mainstay of work was the niche line of providing security and protection to individuals. What that actually entailed would depend on the individual in question. For some, it might be an assessment of their lifestyle, habits and environment to guard against possible kidnap and ransom (KNR). For others it might be the provision of specialist teams to provide real, round-the-clock protection against actual KNR or any other threat that might come up. Some simply liked to have bodyguards draped around like fashion accessories. The people in question included heads of multi-national corporations, celebrities, high net-worth individuals (rich folk to you and me) and even minor royals. If I felt like I was entering a new world going into fancy bars in Mayfair, this was a whole other experience.

Part of my job became to assist in the security assessments and suggest changes if necessary. Naturally, I would look at the IT side of things, examining things like their home WiFi and computer choices. If someone can break into a target's IT they could potentially break into their calendar or email. Getting access to someone's schedule makes them much easier to kidnap. At that time, lots of people still installed their WiFi at home with no security enabled, so it didn't take much to raise the bar quite a bit.

The main issue for me in improving IT security was that most of the individuals we worked for seemed fairly illiterate, from a technical point of view. I could install the world's best firewall, but if it was so complicated to use that someone just unplugged it, then it would become useless. I would therefore have to chat to the individual (if that was even allowed) to determine their skill level and appetite for such things before making any sort of recommendation.

Not being allowed to speak to the individual was something that happened quite regularly. I was, frankly, too far beneath them to be worth speaking to. I was never offended by that although I was unimpressed by one lady who insisted we walk around her house wearing medical-style blue plastic socks so we didn't taint her floor. She kept a stock of them in a drawer ready for unclean visitors such as myself.

While looking at IT security was interesting, it wasn't as much fun as helping Mark and Baz in their part of the assessment. When leaving the military after a long service, it's possible to be retrained before entering 'civvy-street'. Mark had attended a course in TSCM (Technical Surveillance Counter Measures) somewhere overseas - that's sweeping for bugs to you and me. And by bugs, we're talking listening devices, not wildlife.

After the course, he'd been offered a complete set of TSCM kit to purchase and as part of his arrangement with Olive, they'd bought the kit on his behalf. I can't remember if Baz had also been on a course, or just figured it all out, but between the two of them, they were the experts. I was very much the junior team member when it came to TSCM, but could still usefully contribute to a 'sweep'.

TSCM isn't at all like in the movies. In a film, James Bond would enter a room and wave a small box around, equipped with a red light. Within a minute he'd find and extract half a dozen bugs. In reality, it takes hours to sweep even a single room.

There are two main ways to track down a bug. You can either catch it broadcasting or you can try to detect the physical unit. The former is more technical but the latter does actually involve a device with a red light and a lot of time waving it around, somewhat more diligently than Bond would have done. Waving a device around while watching for a red light was within my skill set, so I would go along and assist in this manner. This left Mark and Baz to tackle the more skilled tasks.

Once the initial glamour of pretending to be some sort of spy wore off, assisting in the sweeps themselves wasn't that exciting really. What made it interesting was the locations. Luxuriously appointed Marble Arch townhouses or fancy City boardrooms were all places I was unlikely to set foot otherwise. But by far my favourite location was a luxurious penthouse apartment overlooking the Thames and owned by a fabulously wealthy prince from somewhere in the Middle East.

Olive had a team of four on rotation looking after the 'Arab Prince' as he was described to me. By all accounts, he was a nightmare to protect. He didn't seem to care about being kidnapped and made absolutely no effort to kerb his lifestyle in order to reduce his own risk. He would head into London, hit some fancy nightclub and then invite a hoard of people (including many that he didn't actually know) back to his pad. The protection team would then have to try and circle around discreetly while still providing some sort of useful protection.

Most rotating teams looked after their clients for two weeks on and then had two weeks off. Thus a team of four would only have two with the client at any time. The Arab Prince led such a hectic lifestyle that this was reduced to a weekly rotation to give the team members a chance to recover before they collapsed. Although the team did their best to be professional and do their job, it seemed like they were, in fact, just another expensive accessory that the Prince wanted around, rather than something he actually felt he needed.

As yet another excellent way of spending a lot of money, we were brought in to perform a sweep of his home (or one of his homes, probably). Sweeps are often done outside regular hours. For offices, it's better done while no one else is there to get in the way or for us to be observed. For homes, we tended to work around the client's schedule, again to do the work while they were out. This could also lead to some odd schedules.

It's also important to try and arrive discreetly. If the target really is bugged, there's a fair chance that they are under routine observation as well. Bugs can be harder to find if they've been temporarily disabled, so we didn't want to alert anyone that we were just about to hunt around for them.

I'm not sure we did well at the discreet arrival bit really. All the kit was in quite a number of sizeable Peli cases, heavyweight, solid plastic transport boxes that looked anything but subtle. And if Mark and Baz didn't immediately look like ex-military personnel, they didn't exactly look like that wasn't a distinct possibility either. With some young, nerdy lad in tow obviously. If someone was watching out for a possible sweep team, our arrival would have made them suspicious immediately.

We'd also avoid talking about the sweep while we did one, again because someone might be listening as we were there and turn the devices off remotely. We'd turn a radio on, partly to cover our own noise and partly to aid discovery. The bit of the sweep I was less involved with was trying to discover bugs by their transmissions. A fancy bit of kit would go across a wide spectrum looking for unusual broadcasts. Using the radio helped with this, as the station would be rebroadcast on an unexpected frequency for us to pick up.

For those trying to plant a bug, power is probably the biggest consideration after concealment. Many bugs have a battery as this makes them a lot more portable. But it also limits the lifespan unless the battery is pretty big, in which case it becomes increasingly difficult to hide. Things like golf trophies have been used in the past very successfully; the weight of the batteries in the base wouldn't seem out of place and they often find their way to people's desks which is likely just where the attacker would want them to be.

Other devices rely on being plugged in and usually these masquerade as a regular device, such as a phone charger or even just a multi-socket adapter. The attacker tries their best to get the device into hands of the victim in the hope that they'll place it or plug it in themselves. This is much easier than trying to gain access yourself, although some luck is involved.

For the Arab Prince, we arrived at his apartment in the evening while he was out, presumably somewhere suitably ostentatious. It was a penthouse apartment covering the top three floors of a prominent, riverside tower in central London. It remains the most amazing personal property I've been to. The thing about being rich is it doesn't just buy amazing properties. It also gets you interior designers, teams of decorators and furniture specifically chosen to coordinate with and fit into a given room. This is quite unlike any house I've owned, where the furniture is a mixture of old and new, good quality and otherwise, and definitely not bought with any cohesive plan in mind. However, it wasn't the successful interior design plan that marked this property out against others I'd visited. It was the sheer scale and location that made it amazing. I think mostly I just enjoyed the views. The kitchen had a patio on two sides looking out onto the Thames and some of London's most iconic landmarks. Money can't buy you everything, but it can buy you a really nice view.

A few months later the contract for the Prince's security team ended abruptly. Perhaps the security detail provided to him didn't match his latest colour scheme.

Planting and using any sort of surveillance device without full disclosure is illegal. But that's clearly what bugs are for. Despite the potential for illegal misuse, you can buy bugs quite easily online or even at one or two specialist shops where you can just walk in and pick your favourite flavour. These shops get away with this by selling them as 'for fun only'. Obviously how they are used is up to the end-customer, the shop turns a very deliberate blind eye.

If, during our sweeps, we were to find a bug, it must be left in place and not disturbed further. It could then be reported as a crime and left for the police to examine as a crime scene.

A couple of years after I'd finished working for Olive, one of our former clients was bugged and the fallout from that discovery became rather public. A former business partner had managed to bug her home office and the whole affair ended up in court, as well as splashed all over the papers.

CHAPTER FIVE

22 friends and counting

Olive naturally made good use of their SAS roots for discreet marketing purposes. It was certainly effective and prospective punters usually lapped it up, particularly when delivered with just a whiff of secrecy.

The original founders were Johnny, JY and Dougie. All three had come from the UK Special Forces but in most ways, couldn't have been more different from each other.

Dougie was a quiet Scotsman, tall and fairly thin. He came across as an old-school gentleman and was always friendly to me. Beyond that, I didn't really have much interaction with Dougie and I got the impression that he was the least involved in running the business.

JY, while also Scottish, was an entirely different character to Dougie. More my kind of height (that is to say, on the low side of average) and built like the proverbial brick outhouse. JY was fun, fierce and not to be messed with. That's not to say I didn't try to throw a friendly insult his way on the odd occasion. JY came into the office one morning brandishing photos of a new Audi convertible he'd bought. "What do you think of that?" he asked me. "It looks like a mid-life crisis" I responded without thinking too much, then armed myself with a nervous smile while wondering if I might have pushed him slightly too far. He grumbled and stomped off, but I kept my teeth.

Of the three, JY was probably the one that looked after me the most. I'll stop somewhat short of calling him a father figure, but he was certainly fatherly towards me. In the kind of tough-love manner only a military man (or veteran) can dispense. For example, on the morning of my first trip into the desert (more on this later), I was feeling well-prepared when JY called me over for a once-over and for a few words of advice. Only he didn't get that far.

"What the fuck have you got on your feet?".

"Er, sandals" I replied.

"What use are those if you have to run for it in the desert under fire?".

He had a point!

The last man in the original Olive triangle was Johnny. He was another category of bonkers altogether. He was tall, good looking and always full of energy. Johnny was full of energy to the point where he didn't seem to need as much sleep as most 'regular' humans. It was like a superpower. I've known plenty of people that could pull all-nighters on occasions. Even for a few days running if necessary. But Johnny was one of those rare individuals that could survive indefinitely on three to four hours of sleep. I found it unnatural. He would be at work at his desk long into the night and then get a few hours' sleep under it. Literally under his desk!

While I admired his work ethic, it was a pain when you had to work on anything with him. It was hard to keep up. On one occasion we worked together on a project for a couple of hours in the morning before the office got started. Then again for most of the evening when regular office hours had finished. Obviously, on top of our respective day jobs. At the end of the week I was beaten, but Johnny was still going, despite the fact that he'd been pulling even longer hours than me. I went home for the weekend to sleep. He probably didn't.

Johnny had a delightful way with words. On arriving in the office, I'd typically be greeted with something rude, usually dick related. "Thou art hung like a tiny shrew" or similar. Sort of false prose, vaguely Shakespearean but with a lot less art or subtlety. While this might sound like casual bullying (and I guess to some it might be), he was often the target of his own abuse, with self-deprecating comments about the size of his own nose (large) or manhood (small). Offensive it might have been, but in some ways, I miss that kind of banter.

One of my favourite episodes from this period was an attack on my dress sense. Or perhaps just my clothing budget. After a meeting on The Embankment, my colleague was chatting to me.

"Where did you get that suit from?" I was asked.

"Burtons" came the honest response.

"Well you look like shit. I'm afraid that's not going to cut it in London".

And with that, we jumped into a taxi. I was whisked along to Harvey Nichols in Knightsbridge and taken to the menswear department. There I was forcibly outfitted with an expensive Paul Smith suit together with a shirt, tie and pair of boots.

While I was delighted with my more up-market appearance, this was all looking a bit pricey. I shouldn't have worried as it all went on the company card and I was grinning like a Cheshire Cat. As an aside, the suit didn't last all that long (perhaps the problem stemmed from only having one good suit to wear) but I still have the shoes. They don't look their best anymore, but they still looked good enough when I got married, almost a decade after they were bought. Genuine quality really does pay for itself apparently. Particularly when someone else is paying.

PART THREE

THE MIDDLE EAST

CHAPTER SIX

Shifting sands

After about only six months with Olive, two things happened. Although unrelated, they combined to turn my working life around quite comprehensively.

The decision was made to close the office in Hereford. We were all offered posts in London, with a pay rise to cover additional costs. Having just got started with my new career, I didn't feel like stopping already, so I accepted the change in location.

Mark and Baz had other ideas though, and chose to leave Olive altogether, instead heading off to set up their own business. The technical team changed from three to me overnight.

I didn't fancy becoming a semi-permanent resident of the office in Mayfair. Apart from anything else, the microwave diet didn't really appeal. Luckily one of the other team members stepped in to rescue me. A more recent hire called JC had a flat in Chelsea and offered to rent his spare room to me.

As time goes by the more I realise what a big favour JC did me. I paid him the paltry sum of £350 per month for that room which probably should have been at least quadruple that, if only for the address. The flat was more than an address though, and was a great place to call my base. Apart from a crazy neighbour in the flat underneath, it was pretty perfect. It was also within walking distance of the office. I really like the Tube, but it's hell during the busy periods and walking about an hour each day did me a lot of good.

I now officially both worked and lived in London, although I was still returning to Hereford most weekends where I had a house and my social circle.

The other thing that happened was more newsworthy, at least as far as the rest of the world was concerned. The second Gulf War started. Given that some of the Olive team had been there before and knew the ropes, Olive won a contract to look after the Sky News team in Iraq, mostly in and around Baghdad. Initially this had little impact on me, but fairly quickly (and in fairness, without my noticing at first), the company focus shifted eastwards. And south a bit.

As well as being on the ground in Iraq, we also opened up an office in Kuwait. And by office I mean office, accommodation and everything else in one space, as per usual.

The war in Iraq lasted a mere six weeks until President Bush boldly, and rather rashly, declared "Mission Accomplished". Officially, the conflict had finished and the reconstruction of Iraq had begun. Companies doing the actual reconstruction were lining up to go into Iraq and they needed security teams to keep them safe. Olive was well placed to step up by virtue of their presence in both Iraq and Kuwait.

This is when the full insanity of the Olive team began to pay off. The first teams from companies looking to get work in Iraq were taking tentative steps over the border from Kuwait. Although the conflict had officially finished, there were still pockets of violence. As you might expect, people were quite nervous about travelling around Iraq and Olive was around to provide assistance. This took the form of actual guarding roles, but also providing in-advance surveys of local conditions on the ground.

To do the surveys, Johnny, JY and others were getting up very early, driving from Kuwait City to the border (a couple of hours) and then driving around the main roads and points of interest of southern Iraq. They would then drive back and write up intelligence reports that would be distributed to existing clients and also used for wooing future clients. It looked as if we had whole teams of people collecting intelligence, others writing reports and then the founders meeting with clients and running the business. In reality, it was a small handful of people doing everything and made us look like a much bigger outfit than we were. Punching above our weight barely covers it. Johnny made good use of his no-sleep superpower.

SSA Marine (then Stevedore Services of America) won the contract to get the southerly port of Umm Qasr up and running again. They then contracted Olive to supply all of the security needs for the operation. At the time, it was a very big deal for Olive, having beaten off competition from more established players in the industry. I have zero doubt that this was down to the incredible efforts of the team and the intelligence reports they produced in those early days.

Until then, my main role had been to support the work for our customers in London and beyond. I also looked after the company IT needs as a minor aside. Looking after the IT for a dozen or so people was not a big deal and didn't really take up much of my time. As Olive started to grow a little faster, more of my time was spent looking after an increasing number of laptops, user accounts and of course, users. For me personally, Olive's own IT began to dominate my daily workload.

CHAPTER SEVEN

Trip one to the desert

As part of the contract to help secure the port, Olive was tasked with a number of peripheral activities, including getting IT and communications up and running. I helped to organise and procure a dozen or so desktop computers, together with a server and all the kit to join it together. The desktops were pretty standard, but the server was specced with a special ruggedised, rack-mount case in order to protect it during transport and in situ. I did some initial configuration in the UK and then it was all boxed up ready to be shipped out to Kuwait.

I remember being pretty nervous about being deployed for the first time, although I was too busy to dwell on it much. When I'd joined the Olive team, I'd hoped for overseas trips, but I'd been thinking more exotic cities and not so many war zones. At that point, working for Olive had taken me overseas only as far as Paris and Gibraltar. Still, I was keen to explore further afield and I was assured that I'd never be in any real danger. I had never bothered to do any sort of gap year adventure and I think at that point I still had an itch to go travelling. This would be a different sort of adventure, with the added bonus that someone else would be paying for my travel.

A couple of days before my flight, someone in the office casually asked me if I'd had all my inoculations.

"Er....no".

"Oh" came the response. "Well, it's probably a bit too late for them to do you any good, but you should still go and have them done anyway. It can't hurt".

Turns out, it can hurt quite a bit. I arranged to have my jabs back in Hereford as I had to go back and pack. Doing so involved explaining to the nurse where in the world I was going, so she could select the appropriate ones. It turned out that her husband was in the SAS, what a coincidence. After that, she couldn't do enough for me, including giving me every useful jab and maybe one or two for luck. Normally these jabs would be spread out over a few weeks, but I had them all in one session. Despite the generous number of jabs, it wasn't sore....to begin with.

The night before I was due to depart, I was so busy packing and checking my kit that I suddenly realised it was quite late in the evening and I'd had nothing to eat. I phoned up my Dad and he was at a local sports club, loitering at the bar with my Stepmum. I asked him if, by chance, they'd also not got around to eating yet. They hadn't so we arranged to meet at a nearby Chinese restaurant.

Even if it was mostly down to bad planning, I was quite pleased that we could all meet up before I went off for a few weeks. However, it turned out to be a pretty miserable meal. The food was fine, but the mood was less than light. Although the war had officially ended, images from the TV of the realities of war were still very fresh in all our minds. The general impression was that I was off, probably never to return and this was less a pre-adventure meal and more of a communal last supper. I tried to be buoyant but I struggled to enjoy myself.

As a parent now myself, I realise the difference in attitude I have towards my kids' wellbeing compared to my own. I don't think you can really grasp this until you become a parent yourself. I can't blame them for the miserable meal that evening, it can't have been fun for them, considering where I was going to. But it certainly increased my sense of foreboding.

Thanks to the generous number of jabs I'd received, by the time I got on the plane the next day, I felt like I'd been kicked in the arms by horses. My poor punctured muscles were complaining in the most bruising fashion and trying to get some rest on the overnight flight was challenging.

I must have looked a sight when I stepped off the plane in Kuwait City. One of the guys in the office had convinced me that I should look the part of a seasoned and accomplished business traveller. As such, I'd been cajoled into wearing a linen suit that I owned but had rarely worn. Apart from the dubious styling, the sleeves were just slightly too long for me which was probably why it usually languished in the cupboard. I must have looked like I'd mugged 'The Man From Del Monte' and then lost his hat.

Kuwait airport was dripping in marble and awash with air conditioning. I thought it looked smart and upmarket, both words that didn't describe me in my ridiculous attire as I trundled nervously along towards the man in the booth.

I'm pretty sure the guard at passport control cared a lot more about the validity of my passport and visa than he did my suit. Regardless of what smoothed my entry into the country, I was soon reunited with my luggage and strolled through to the arrivals area. JY was there to meet me and we had a relaxing drink in a coffee shop while we chatted. Odd the things you recall, but I distinctly remember having a cinnamon bun with too much icing on the top. It was delicious and partly made up for being up at around 5am with sore shoulders and not a great deal of sleep.

JY drove me to the local Olive HQ. This was a large flat which was being used to service all of Olive's needs. The living room was also the main office space and one (or more) of the bedrooms had bunkbeds in them to cram more people in. It was far from exotic but I was enjoying myself immensely. My head was swimming from the excitement of a new and unfamiliar country and probably the overly sugared breakfast.

It was here that I was introduced to Lee, who I would be working with on this project. Lee was a bit different to most of the other Olive recruits that I'd met thus far in that he was about my age. Almost everyone else had at least ten years on me. He'd also been in 264 SAS Signal Squadron but that hadn't quite worked out for him and he'd ended up on civvy street a lot sooner than he'd planned. Lee had more than a bit of fun, cowboy attitude about him which came in very handy.

Our kit landed in Kuwait not long after we did but somehow got stuck in customs. Not only was it stuck, but it didn't seem to be coming out in a hurry. This was obviously a problem but not one that I had any idea how to fix. Lee didn't seem phased though and soon enough I found myself with him at some Kuwaiti government office trying to find the right person to talk to. We trailed around, chatting to people until we found someone suitably high up and with the authority to release our kit. Lee was able to turn on the charm enough to get the appropriate signature which unlocked our previously impounded gear.

What I remember most about this excursion was an odd moment with a more junior member of staff. As we waited around in various places for people to become available, we were left in the company of some of the Kuwaiti nationals.

One chap spoke excellent English so I tried to chat to him a little. I asked him about the local cuisine and if there was some sort of national dish. He went into some detail for me to describe something that sounded suspiciously like a kebab.

"Sounds great", I said, "Would you recommend it?".

"No", came the response. So much for national culinary pride.

Eventually we managed to get all the kit back to our office. Or at least outside the front door. It was too much to take upstairs and we arranged for another courier to collect it and travel with us across the border. I got lumped with waiting outside for a while to make sure nothing got stolen. While I'd been there for a few days at that point, this was my first chance to truly experience the desert heat in the middle of the day. Despite being in the shade and moving very little, I was knackered and dripping with sweat inside forty-five minutes.

Eventually we loaded up again and set off enjoying the very welcome delights of aircon with a lorry carrying all the gear following behind. We drove the two hours or so through the desert to the border crossing. The most southerly official border crossing into Iraq is called Abdali (on the Kuwaiti side). It's about half an hour from there to Umm Qasr. There was also a military-only crossing much closer to Umm Qasr which saved driving time and therefore reduced the chances of being attacked. Somehow Olive had successfully negotiated passage despite us not being part of the military force, which was a real help. All we had to do was show our 'official' Olive ID cards to get across. These cards were being produced back at the Kuwaiti office with a regular printer and a laminator. I still have my old ID in a drawer somewhere. How it was ever considered official looking enough to allow international travel beats me.

The Kuwaiti side of the border was reasonably smart. There were long fences disappearing into the distance on either side with large sliding gates blocking the road. Armed guards remained in their air-conditioned hut until we approached and then they came out to check us out. The Iraqi checkpoint was after a short drive through a section of "no-man's land". It was distinctly less formal although all the required elements were present, such as barbed wire and giant concrete blocks to make it look suitably unfriendly and impassable other than past the guard. One chap dressed in a scruffy t-shirt manned a small booth which gave shade but certainly no air con. He gave a cursory glance at our ID and then lifted the single arm blocking our path. And with that simple crossing, I was in Iraq. I've had more difficulty gaining entry to car parks.

We'd radioed ahead and someone was at the border crossing to meet us, partly to show us the rest of the way and partly to hand over a weapon to Lee. We continued the drive to Umm Qasr, still followed by a driver with his lorry and all the computer kit. The short journey took us past an old, abandoned UN complex and along the edge of the local town. Once past this, we went along a short section of main road and into the port itself.

I can't say the port was a big surprise to me. I don't think I had any significant pre-conceptions about what a port should look like, so it was all just new. Umm Qasr was (and probably still is) Iraq's only deep-water port, capable of getting any significant sized boats (and therefore decent volumes of shipping) in and out. It was also the only port capable of allowing large military naval vessels to dock.

Iraq didn't have any sort of navy to protect its shores so when the war had started it made an impressive strategic decision. As it couldn't really defend its shores, its main fear was that the UK or USA would dock an enormous ship and allow troops and gear to easily disembark. To prevent this, the Iraqis had scuppered a lot of ships in the dock area, making the whole port area a massive hazard to any incoming vessels.

The port was therefore not actually very active with 'normal' port activity. There were massive storage warehouses but these remained stubbornly empty. Shipping containers were stacked up, but not in use or going anywhere. Most of the activity, apart from setting up necessary infrastructure, was for teams of specialists performing wreck removal. Most admired amongst these were the divers that worked in the murky depths. They used specialist cutting equipment capable of cutting up the wrecks underwater to be lifted out in chunks. Apparently it was very dangerous work and presumably suitably well paid. There were also small crane boats to go with them which were capable of lifting the separated chunks of boat out of the water. They looked like a large catamaran with a lifter attached. Occasionally one of the boats was small enough to be lifted out whole, which was quite a sight. The boats, or bits of boats, would be dumped on the dock to be repaired or just cut up further. It looked like a boat graveyard and the wrecks were both fascinating and eerie.

While the lack of easy access via the water might have been an inconvenience, it had certainly not prevented there from being a significant military presence. Both the British and American military had teams based within the port. The port's existing walls provided a starting point for basic security and the small road network within gave a layout to build around. They'd positioned themselves behind the main entrance to the port, blocking it off for their own use. We had to gain access via the smaller north gate instead, along with everyone else.

SSA, the company now running the port, had taken over a

warehouse near to the north gate and this had become their centre of operations. To provide additional protection, a circle of shipping containers had been placed around the warehouse, with a small gap providing controlled access in and out. It was like Lego, but on a slightly larger scale. The warehouse and the safe space created around it was to become home during my visits.

Within the warehouse were a large number of smaller buildings. They were using the larger building like a giant sunshade, with a scrappier version of a holiday camp inside. The smaller buildings were flat-roofed Portakabin style, and they fulfilled a variety of roles. A few were used as offices and a couple for social needs with TVs and sofas. The largest building housed the mess hall and kitchen. The rest and by far the most numerous were cabins used for accommodation.

The type of room you got depended on a couple of factors, but primarily the type of contract you were on. The support staff (cooks, cleaners etc) were lowest in the pecking order. Next up were the Gurkhas (more on them later) and then the remaining SSA or Olive staff were perilously placed at the top and therefore got the best rooms. Until I'd been invited to wander around and look in a few other cabins, I didn't realise the disparity between everyone.

Each cabin was split into two halves and each half had just a largish room and a dedicated bathroom with a sink, shower and toilet. The Gurkhas and support staff were crammed in, with a lot of them sharing each room using bunk beds. I can't remember how many were squeezed in, but it was very cramped. In comparison, I had a room to myself with a queen-sized bed, a desk and so on. In my defence, I did actually work in there quite a bit of the time so it wasn't entirely without justification. But it still felt a little unfair.

That's not to say things were perfect, even with your own room and they all certainly came with their fair share of quirks. Firstly, the warehouse had never been designed with modern plumbing in mind. To deal with the waste from the toilets and showers, a soil pipe had been run behind each row of cabins with a vertical vent pipe behind every second cabin. The issue was that the vertical pipes weren't very tall, and high temperatures meant that there was quite a bit of venting going on. Sadly, the top of the pipe lined up quite neatly with the external part of the air-conditioning unit. If you were unlucky enough to get one of these rooms you could either enjoy cold air that smelt of shit or turn the smelly air con off and melt. It was a tough choice! Later when I returned on future trips, the first thing I did when assigned a cabin was to go behind and see if I'd been given a stinky one.

The bathrooms were individually equipped with mini-water heaters for the showers. If we turned them on, we risked them exploding when combined with the ambient temperature. Luckily, it wasn't necessary to turn them on and a warm or occasionally cool shower was pretty pleasant.

Looking back, I have no recollection where all the foulness from the pipes went to. Things like food and fresh water were driven in, so I guess the turds were driven back out. Hopefully it wasn't all just dumped in the sea.

Lee and I spent the next week or so setting things up. It wasn't just 'my' IT gear that needed installing. Lee had already made a start, but was still busy installing a lot of different equipment related to communications. There were short distance, hand-held radios (fancy walkie-talkies to me) and a couple of large satellite dishes to connect us up to the internet. I helped Lee with the radios and satellite dishes and he helped me with the IT kit. Some of the gear was installed within the offices in the warehouse but most of it went to one of the larger buildings in the port which was used by some of the local admin staff. At least that was the plan, but at the time it was empty most of the time, probably because the port was then still largely shut down. Regardless, we diligently set everything up and (if I do say so myself) we did a pretty good job of it.

Once the internet connection was up and running, I setup WiFi, so suddenly everyone with a laptop could get online. I'm sure that made me pretty popular. WiFi is so ubiquitous nowadays that it's easy to forget that in 2003 it was still just getting started.

Despite my best planning, things always change and inevitably we found ourselves short of a few bits and pieces. We couldn't exactly pop to a nearby shop, but finding equipment was reasonably okay. In London there's an area on and around Tottenham Court Road that's awash with techie shops, selling computers, cameras, hi-fi and so on. It's a great place where a savvy buyer can pick up a genuine bargain and a mug can be rightfully fleeced. Kuwait City has its own Tottenham Court Road, although I forget its name. I really enjoyed going there, typically in the evening to avoid the heat. More than in London, there was constant hustle and bustle, plus the opportunity to score a bargain.

In London the many shops were, as would seem obvious, in direct competition with each other. In Kuwait, however, they seemed both in competition and collaboration with each other. It didn't matter which shop you went into, they always had everything in stock. In reality, when you asked for something they didn't have, they would pop to a neighbouring shop and take what they had, presumably for a reasonable share of the profit. It was quite comical when the staff member said they were going to their stock room, but you could clearly see them go out of their back door and into the next shop along.

It was great to explore both Kuwait and Iraq during my first trip, which must have lasted around three weeks in total. Inevitably, my work was finally completed and I flew back to

London, happy, alive and possibly sporting a reasonable sun tan.

CHAPTER EIGHT

What's your Locstat?

Things in Iraq were starting to hot up, pun intended. As the new-normal settled in and American dollars started flowing to more reconstruction projects, more companies inevitably joined the party. All individuals arriving to do the work needed protection and companies like Olive were happy to offer their services. While demand for protection was growing, there was a finite number of suitably experienced people to provide it. This led to increasing rates of pay as companies fought over a limited pool of talent and some would naturally jump between companies in search of better pay.

When I left Umm Qasr, I wasn't expecting to be returning very soon. Olive was contractually obliged to provide someone capable of maintaining all the kit and providing ongoing support. Lee was going to do this, and did so very capably. Unfortunately for us, Lee was tempted by bigger dollars elsewhere. Due to accumulated leave and his short notice period, he was gone almost as soon as he'd made the decision and that left Olive with a bit of problem, from a contractual point of view.

Given that I understood at least half of the system pretty

well, along with having some experience of the location, I was the number one choice to go in as a stand-in. This was lucky, as there actually wasn't anyone else.

"Don't worry" said Simon, our Head of Recruitment, "it should only take a couple of weeks to find your replacement and then you can come home again".

I repeated the same route as before, flying from London to Kuwait City and then driving over the border into Iraq. On arrival at the port, I was handed a radio and left to my own devices. I went off to explore the place again and check to see how all the kit was fairing. I was busy minding my own business when a call came over the open channel on the radio.

"Graeme, what's your Locstat?"

I just about knew how to work the radio, but I had zero idea how to respond to this question. I pressed the button on the side of the radio and responded rather nervously with "What's a Locstat?".

"Location and status". Oh right, that made some sense.

"I'm over in the main operations building and er...... I'm just fine thanks."

"Get your arse back to the warehouse, it's brew time."

The problem with radios, as you might know, is that everyone with a radio gets to hear what everyone else is saying. I had arrived as the expert to look after, amongst other things, all the radios. But from one brief exchange, I'd managed to prove to those listening in that I didn't even know basic lingo. My stock as the new resident expert had just plummeted.

It was true though. I could just about use the radio (even if

I didn't know the right terminology) but I had no idea how to commission a new one or fix a broken unit.

Despite the relatively short period of time, a significant number of staff had already moved onto other projects. The job at Umm Qasr was relatively safe and stable. Some of the more experienced staff had been moved onto contracts in the more hostile areas and fresh faces had filled the gaps. So most of the credit I'd built up on my first visit had been lost as I was new to a lot of the team.

Still, I thought, I only have to be here a couple of weeks and then I'll be off again. As long as nothing too serious goes wrong, I should be fine!

CHAPTER NINE

Motivation is a dish best served empty

Sadly, there was more to go wrong in Umm Qasr. The other thing I was not an expert in was the satellite dishes.

The internet connection had stopped working a few days prior to my arrival and in their desperation, one or two bright sparks had taken matters into their own hands. On the assumption that a desert storm might have moved the dish, they'd tried 'wiggling it around a bit'. It hadn't helped.

Satellite dishes that receive only, like the ones attached to your house for TV, don't have to be all that accurate when it comes to the direction they face. However, most dishes that send as well as receive have to be a lot more accurate. As I later read in the manual, one millimetre out on the ground equates to roughly one kilometre out in the sky.

Armed with the manual and little other clue, I set off trying to figure out what to do. These days I'd probably be able to access an alternative method of getting online and then watch a how-to video on Youtube. Back then, I was largely on my own.

One morning on probably the second or third day of struggling, the big cheese from SSA came in to ask me how I was getting on.

"Not so well," I explained, "This is my first satellite dish."

He seemingly thought the problem was motivation rather than lack of knowledge, so he attempted to help me out. Perhaps he thought I'd been playing Minesweeper.

"The canteen is out of bounds for you until this is fixed."

What?!

Those that know me personally would know this is not the best way to get good work out of me. If I'm ever in a meeting that trails on past 1pm, I stop thinking about anything other than escaping to get some lunch. Even more so if it's a buffet lunch waiting for us in the room on a trolley. Stop droning on, I want to eat!

Instead of focusing on the problem, I was now panicking about what I was going to do without food. The others nearby reassured me that he was just kidding, so when I still hadn't sorted it out by lunchtime, I went to the canteen anyway, hoping I wouldn't actually be barred. I wasn't but I didn't enjoy that meal much as I ducked down and tried to look inconspicuous.

The problem, it turned out, was with the equipment I had to hand. Or my lack of understanding of how it worked. I had figured out which direction the dish should be pointing (both left to right and up and down). When that was done, I needed to hone in on the exact spot by using a little detector which could be plugged in as needed. This would flash a red light and beep when it locked on to the correct satellite. Yes, I was back to waving around things I didn't really understand while waiting for a red light.

Only it turned out that the little detector would happily beep at ANY satellite it locked on to, not just the one I wanted. This explained why I would repeatedly think that success was in the bag only to find that yet again, nothing actually happened. I was at a loss for a solution.

Luckily, our canteen came to the rescue, in a fashion.

"Why don't you ask some of the army guys to help you? They've got lots of dishes."

I can't remember who made the suggestion, but they were right. The British Army had all sorts of equipment and experts within the port and there was almost certainly someone who could help. The problem would be, as far as I could see, getting their support. Why would they bother to help us? I voiced my concerns and received another excellent insight.

"Don't worry about that, they'll do anything for a good lunch"

It turns out that was perfectly accurate. The British Army had a reasonable canteen, but ours (the SSA's) was distinctly better. And if you've been eating in the same place for ages, just different was also a bonus. We had a good and varied menu each day, as well as luxuries like a fridge full of soft drinks and a small freezer that was occasionally stocked with ice cream. I set off across to the port to the British camp, taking someone along with me who 'knew a bloke'. With that starting point, we wandered around until we found someone willing to help with only the promise of a free lunch to trade. It worked a treat.

Not only did they know what they were doing, they also brought with them a detector that could be targeted to alert only when the dish was pointing at the correct satellite. It was probably sorted within half an hour. As soon as the dish was pointed accurately in the right place, everything burst into life and normality was restored along with my canteen privileges.

Bizarrely, this wasn't the only time I was on the receiving end of food-related hostility. On a later trip, when I could be considered an old hand, I was chatting to a small group during a tea break. One chap that I didn't know wandered in and headed straight for me. He clearly felt that I must be the new boy, so our respective positions in the pecking order needed to be established.

"Hey new boy, make me a cup of tea"

He was massive and carrying an AK-47. Now I know that he's not actually going to shoot me there and then in the canteen, but regardless of logic, it's still pretty intimidating.

In truth, I don't actually drink tea, although I'm still happy to take a tea break. Plus, the aforementioned fridge provided me with unlimited fizzy drinks and fruit juice. So while the rest of the blokes quite happily made each other tea, I opted out of that role on the grounds that they wouldn't ever be able to return the favour. No one had ever complained about this to me, despite it being quite odd not to drink tea if you're in the army. But of course, I had never been in the army, and they probably just regarded it as yet another amusing quirk of 'the civvy'. Not this time though.

"I don't drink tea so I don't make it" I said, with only a slight quiver in my voice. "Sorry."

"I didn't ask you if YOU drank tea, I told you to make ME a cup!" he roared in return.

I knew this was one of those make or break moments. If I relented and made him a tea, I'd lose face in front of everyone else. And I'd be tea bitch to him and probably everyone else for the duration of my trip.

"No," I said as bravely as I could possibly muster, "I'm not making your tea".

He stomped off to make his own tea leaving me to visibly relax. The rest of the group silently nodded and smiled at me. I'd done the right thing and earned myself just a tiny bit of kudos as well.

CHAPTER TEN

The best babysitters in the world

Apart from the guy in the canteen making hot-beverage-related demands plus one or two others, I was actually incredibly well looked after. Despite working with all the ex-military guys in London, I felt the gulf between us was larger when I was operating in their environment. They were generally older and always a lot more experienced whereas I was young, looked even younger and was entirely green when it came to surviving in hostile environments.

One of my worries when I was first deployed was that I would be treated like a numpty. Given that I'd tried to enter Iraq for the first time wearing flip-flops, this wasn't exactly undeserved.

In reality, I was treated like 'someone that doesn't know anything', but actually in a really positive way. Everyone looked after me well, took me under their wing and I really felt like I was under their protection. Not only that, but some would go out of their way to try to expand my experience rather than simply put me in a safe but boring corner.

On one occasion, we diverted while driving along the desert, off-road and into what (to me at least) looked like featureless and endless sand. After ten or fifteen minutes we came across a series of large guns, old and abandoned. Apparently, they were relics from the Iran/Iraq conflict and were still pointing towards the Iranian border. The guys I was with happily explained the guns to me and the context of why they were there. They also took some photos of me standing in front of the guns, insisting that I had a rifle slung over my shoulder just for effect.

"That'll scare the shit out of your parents," they chuckled.

Looking back, I also took more than a couple of unnecessary risks in the interest of exploration. One day I accompanied a couple of guys on a trip to a nearby American base. We went to get lunch and to shop in the PX, an American store selling treats to military personnel while overseas. I bought a heavily discounted Leatherman but they refused to sell me a grey t-shirt with 'ARMY' written on the front. The sort you've probably seen in movies. Apparently you actually had to be in the American Army to be allowed one of those. Spoilsports! It would have made a great souvenir.

Our canteen was good, but the one on the American base was superb. They had far more on offer and I could have happily eaten there for weeks without having the same thing twice. That said, I'm not sure the food was so good that it was worth the additional risk, but maybe it was for the experience. The driver on that excursion was later killed by an IED on a similar road elsewhere in Iraq. I still feel sad about that. I also feel bad that I can't actually remember his name, which doesn't feel sufficiently respectful for someone that helped to keep me alive.

CHAPTER ELEVEN

The port

Back in Umm Qasr, evenings were almost always a team affair. Not that you couldn't hide away if you felt like it. There was a TV room where we would typically consume box sets or films. It's odd how circumstances can change your opinion or mood. I'd watched a couple of episodes of the show Phoenix Nights back in the UK and hated it. When I tried it again in the TV room, it was fantastic. I'm not sure if it was the company or the limited alternatives that made it much improved from my first viewing.

Actually, getting hold of stuff to watch wasn't too tricky. A few enterprising locals had set up a 'shop' within the port to sell pirate DVDs to anyone with dollars to spare. In fact, it didn't matter what you bought, the price was always the same: a dollar a disc. The shop itself was a shipping container fitted out with some sofas and DVDs covering all the walls. They'd even got a TV installed so you could test the discs to make sure they worked before taking them away. I have no idea where they were drawing the electricity from. In some cases they had stuff for sale which was only just in the cinemas in the UK. Some of their releases weren't exactly perfect though. Some films had multiple sets of subtitles on-screen covering different languages. One copy of Star Wars that we watched had auto-generated English subtitles as well as two other languages. The wording was so wrong to be hilarious, but very distracting as a result.

Although the south of Iraq was under the control of the Brits (with the Yanks controlling the North), the entire country was run on dollars. This was true everywhere, from the black markets to the legit shops within the bases. I found it odd, but this even extended to the British run shop aimed mainly at British Service personnel.

If we wanted to venture slightly further than our own warehouse, the British Camp within the port had a couple of bars we could try. One was run by the Army and the other by the RAF. They both had the same two-can rule: you could buy a maximum of two cans per night and they were opened for you at the bar to avoid stockpiling. If you went up to buy a round, you had to identify who the drinks were for. The bar staff would try and keep track and they were remarkably good at it considering the number of people sitting around on any given evening. As per the other shops, the bar only took dollars and it was a dollar per can, regardless of what you had.

There is almost nothing in life as satisfying as a cold beer in the desert. In the evening, the temperature was still high but far more bearable than during the middle of the day. It was fantastic and we probably went over for a beer about once per week.

We would chat amongst ourselves and occasionally tried to make friends (or at least make conversation) with some of the military folk. I even bumped into someone I knew from Hereford once or twice.

The Army weren't allowed to visit the RAF bar and vice versa. This was to prevent cheating the two-can rule and probably because they couldn't be trusted to play nicely. We were allowed into both bars though, and with a little care to avoid looking like we'd already started drinking, we'd be able to double up on the two-can rule.

Although it was only about a ten-minute walk, we'd always drive between our warehouse and the bar. This was apparently for safety reasons; we didn't want to get jumped in the dark. I also think it was because at least one member of the team was too lazy. To be fair, I never voiced any sort of complaint against driving.

It did introduce one interesting aspect though. If we'd managed to sneak in four cans, this put us well over the legal limit for driving in most countries. Not in Iraq though, at least not within the confines of our closed area where we were the closest thing to a local police force. This meant that the main challenge was simply driving the vehicle while inebriated. I acted as designated driver quite regularly. Not that I stayed sober, simply that I was designated 'still capable of driving reasonably well while under the influence'. Not only did I happily drive back, but there would often be calls from the back seats to take detours, over rough terrain and so on. I cheerfully obliged, although perhaps I was always going to be cheerful and obliging for silly stunts after a few beers.

It did get very out of hand once, although thankfully I wasn't out that night. A group had managed to get one or two more drinks even than the two bars/two cans trick would normally allow. Instead of returning to the warehouse, they had decided it would be fun to leave the relative safety of the port and go speeding up the main road. It didn't end well.

The driver managed to lose control and roll their 4x4. Everyone suffered bumps and bruises and one unlucky adventurer ended up with a broken bone. By the morning they'd managed to get back, sober up and even retrieve the vehicle somehow. They came up with a ridiculous story to explain away their injuries and the vehicle damage. I can't remember the details of their excuse, but it involved chasing down hostiles and was clearly a complete fabrication.

Taking such unnecessary risks should have been an immediate, sackable offence. Their wafer-thin lie held and they kept their jobs, despite everyone seemingly knowing the truth. I think it helped that they had one of the clients with them in the car. Sending them home would have meant admitting that the whole event really happened, which no-one seemed inclined to do. Clearly the client was also keen to keep his job and maintain the lie.

On a shorter trip to the port, I was given someone else's cabin to stay in while they went back to Kuwait for a few days. This meant that they would still have their things in the room, which would normally be empty. When I arrived in the morning, he had yet to leave, so he approached me to give me some important information about his room and its contents. The only issue was that due his thick Northern Irish accent, I was struggling to understand what it was that was so important.

He could see that it wasn't sinking in and as his frustrations increased at my lack of comprehension, so did his volume and the strength of his accent. This culminated in him shouting at me, now in front of a small audience.

"DO YOUZ UNDERSTAND WAAT OIM SAYN?" he bellowed[2].

"Only that last bit" I replied, fairly deadpan.

It was genuinely the only full sentence that I'd managed to grasp. While he seemed on the verge of shaking with rage,

---

[2] Apologies to anyone from Northern Ireland for the blatant butchering of a perfectly lovely accent.

the audience by now were shaking with mirth, which helped to defuse the situation. Someone stepped in to translate and show me what it was I should really be grasping.

The short but incomprehensible message was that I wasn't to touch anything inside a particular cupboard in the room. This wasn't to protect anyone's privacy, but to save my life and potentially anyone else's within the blast radius. It turned out that there was a fully working RPG (rocket propelled grenade) hiding in the cupboard, and under no circumstances was I to fiddle with it. This seemed a fairly reasonable ask. I think I may have peeked at it once or twice, wary that my glance could be enough to set it off.

As I previously mentioned, the canteen was good enough to act as a source of possible bribery. For me at least, on one extended visit, it was a little bit too good.

The menu had a distinctly American lean. This was particularly noticeable at breakfast, where, as well as things like cereal and toast, it was possible to order pancakes with bacon or even waffles with syrup. I was particularly keen on the waffles, although sausage and eggs would also make a routine appearance on my breakfast plate. I still don't understand how pancakes go with bacon. For both lunch and evening meal, it was possible to get a hot meal with a dessert if you fancied it, although lighter options were available. Or so I heard.

Despite the American menu, the cooks were actually Indian and, as well as the western food, they also prepared authentic cuisine for the many Gurkhas that were on site. Because we had more people than space in the canteen, meals were in two shifts with the Gurkhas eating first. This suited me fine, as there was almost always a curry from their menu left over that we could also choose from. I had no idea what I was eating half the time, but it was delicious. One thing to be wary of though was the likely presence of meat bones.

Unlike in the UK where restaurants typically limit themselves to serving chicken breast, these more authentic dishes used a lot more of the bird. It looked like it had simply been chopped into manageable chunks with a massive cleaver. It probably had, and that meant that any bones you might find also frequently had sharp ends. Diners beware!

As you can probably tell from my glowing review, I was quite a fan of the canteen, and after a couple of weeks of over-indulging, it was beginning to show. Trapped in the desert was not the first place you'd expect to put on weight, but I'd managed it.

I decided that I needed to burn off the extra kilos with some exercise, which I'd not been getting a lot of. I mentioned it to a colleague and they said I should try going running with Fat Cat.

Fat Cat had a real name, but it wasn't nearly as novel as his nickname, so we'll stick with that. He had been going out for nightly runs when it had cooled off ever so slightly. I wasn't about to go running by myself through the port so having someone to go with seemed like a good idea.

We set off and it became clear very quickly that Fat Cat was out of my league when it came to running. He would run off ahead of me, turn round and come back, using me as a marker to loop around and then set off ahead of me again. He was literally running circles around me. When we got back, I was knackered. I collapsed into a chair while Fat Cat set about destroying a punch bag he'd setup. The others laughed at me and I was let in on the big joke. It turned out that Fat Cat was a former Physical Training instructor and had previously run circles around people for a living.

I decided that running wasn't for me and looked to the one alternative available to me. Some bright spark had installed a badminton net and painted a court on the floor at one end of the warehouse. The roof to the warehouse did a good job of providing shade during the day and keeping it slightly cooler. But in the evening, the reverse could be true and it could be hotter inside than out, although it was still cooler than it had been in the day. By the early evening it was usually high thirties to early forties centigrade inside the warehouse which is pretty hot before you've even started to do any exercise.

Games of badminton were less about points and more a war of attrition. The game was really to see who would quit first, on the verge of heat exhaustion and therefore forfeit the match. I can't remember how long we played for, it seemed like ages but probably wasn't. I did manage to keep up the badminton for longer than the running, although still not enough to fully counteract the damage done by all the breakfast waffles.

CHAPTER TWELVE

The road to Baghdad

Inevitably, my visits to Iraq weren't going to be limited to Umm Qasr. Olive teams were dotted about in plenty of locations and although I didn't have to support other client projects, I did have to help the Olive teams with their own IT.

We didn't actually have our own offices within Iraq (to my knowledge anyway) and simply took residence within locations controlled by the customers' we were looking after. This was a good arrangement for both parties; we got convenient lodgings and they had their security team living on site.

This was the situation on Shaibah Air Base just outside Basra, although I no longer recall who the customer was. The accommodation was a small compound within the large air base. A fenced-off set of cabins, as within Umm Qasr but without the benefit of a warehouse roof over the top. Yet again, some were designated for sleeping, some for offices and others for communal spaces such as a canteen.

The number of Olive staff based in Shaibah was relatively small, which in turn meant the IT issues stored up for me to fix were few in number. I therefore never spent more than a couple of nights there before returning.

The compound was a bit dull mostly, but the sprawling air base was more interesting. It was spread out over quite a large area with troops from many nations either based there or passing through including British, Dutch, Czech, Danish and Norwegian. I think it was the Norwegians that had stuck a 'No Skiing' sign up outside their camp. Someone must have had to source that sign and ship it to Iraq – serious dedication for quite a silly joke. I thoroughly approved.

We had reasonable liberty to roam around, although, inevitably, some places were off limits. Relatively speaking, Shaibah had excellent facilities for service personnel compared to those in the desert, including a gym and a rock-climbing wall. One novelty was the Pizza Hut 'restaurant'. In reality, it was the back-end of a large truck with a serving hatch and some seating around it. Despite the simplicity of the surroundings, it was a real treat and I enjoyed ordering a massive pizza. I also have a few touristy photos on account of the oddity of the whole situation.

It didn't escape me that prices were kind of similar to what they would have been in the UK. This was strange in itself, as the cost of logistics must have been astronomical. I can only assume it was subsidised as a morale boosting effort. It was doubly weird when you consider that a single large pizza probably cost at least several days wages for the majority of locals.

In February 2004 I was asked to go to Baghdad to take a look at the Olive IT gear in place there. One reason that the kit needed my hands-on touch was that the teams often deployed in such haste that I didn't have time to equip anyone with a configured laptop before they left the UK. Kit would be acquired in Kuwait (or anywhere else) to be used immediately and worry about finer points like anti-virus software later. I did request that we keep a stock of laptops ready to go, but apparently no one wanted to plan or invest that far ahead. Thus I was stuck patching and fixing laptops that I was often meeting for the first time, as well as their owners.

Another reason for needing to sort out laptops was the damage done by pornography. Not directly, obviously, but the viruses that inevitably seemed to accompany the porn. In pretty much any other industry, using your work laptop to view pornography would be bad for your career. At Olive, it was broadly accepted, with the justification that it was unreasonable to question the use of porn when the guys might be killed the next day. While I could understand the position, the reality for me was that I was putting myself in additional risk just to sort out the accompanying problems.

In the run-up to my trip to Baghdad I was in Kuwait, working in the office and ensuring I had enough spare parts to deal with any issues that might possibly crop up. Shaibah might have had a Pizza Hut, but I was pretty sure that PC World hadn't yet made it to Baghdad. It was a long and dangerous way to go back to Kuwait just for a forgotten cable.

Unfortunately while I was there I also managed to catch something and I was pretty ill. I had a temperature high enough to cause hallucinations and had what I believe in medical circles is called 'the shits'. This didn't exactly bode well for a long car journey with zero chance of a public toilet. I was attended to by one of the team who was trained as a medic. He visited reasonably often, equipped with various tablets but little sympathy. Clearly a friendly bedside manner hadn't been included in his mandatory training, or maybe he'd just missed that part.

Although I was obviously keen to recover, there wasn't a big rush for me to get to Baghdad. I wasn't being specially driven there, I would simply catch a lift with one of the crews already going up with a client. This happened two or three times a week, so if I missed my planned ride, I could simply get a lift with the next team. On this occasion, rather than set off directly from Kuwait I was going to go to Shaibah for one night and then get picked up by a team going the rest of the way the next day.

I was plied with enough Imodium pills to bung me up for a week. And limit the chances of a potentially very exposed and dangerous roadside poop.

I was also equipped with body armour and a helmet for the journey. Both came in a variety of sizes, all of which seemed to be too big for me. I have a delightful photo of me trying it all on not long after I'd managed to raise myself from my plague bed. It's generally acknowledged that I look young for my age. In the photo, the combination of recent illness with the oversized body armour makes me look ridiculous. It looks as if Olive was sending the work experience boy into a war zone. Maybe they were! Despite not doing me any favours in the heroics department, it's still one of my favourite photos.

On the planned morning of departure I was feeling fine, so I set off to Basra with my fingers crossed and probably my legs too. The three-hour or so journey was thankfully uneventful and I managed to reach the air base without soiling myself and upsetting the others in the car.

The next morning was an early start. The crew set off, with me sitting in the back with our client. We set off northwards on a journey expected to take around five or six hours.

Regardless of which route you take, the road to Baghdad is long and relentlessly unchanging. Occasionally we'd meet a vast, snaking convoy of military vehicles heading in the other direction, but otherwise the roads were largely clear. In our vehicle, the music also had a repetitive quality about it. It was about the time where CDs were all powerful, but inexplicably, most vehicles still came with a cassette deck.

The supply of cassettes was quite limited so we ended up listening to the same few over and over again. The road to Baghdad had a soundtrack seemingly dominated by Alanis Morisette.

This journey was much longer than anything I had experienced before while in Iraq. Although I was wary of the unknown and increased danger of this longer trip, the combination of seemingly endless amounts of both desert and Alanis sent me to sleep.

As my shoulders didn't quite reach high enough to take the weight when sitting down, the oversized body armour would instead rest on my bladder. It didn't notice it to start with, but after a while I would wake up with a real need to pee and not much opportunity to do so. When we did stop, it was dangerous to be stationary for too long, so we then had to piss with some urgency and then get going again.

It's funny what normal actions become more dangerous in the circumstances. You would never think that it would be risking your life to take a roadside pee, but that was the reality at the time. Other things that I was used to became skewed with a new logic too. We no longer wore seatbelts for example. The reasoning was that if were under attack in a gun fight, you might need to be able to get out of the vehicle as quickly as possible. This was considered a greater danger than the increased chances of injury in the event of a vehicle collision. It was simply a balancing act of the various risks that you faced.

One thing that they did have en route was the equivalent of service stations. These could range in size from a single petrol station (with guards, blockades, etc.) to a sizeable compound. As we were ultimately working on behalf of the coalition forces, we were allowed to use these facilities for free, refuelling the vehicles and ourselves. We could help ourselves to ration packs, which while not usually delicious, were generally pretty interesting to investigate the contents. I liked the fact that regardless of the type of dish in the hot-food ration packs, there was always a sizeable portion of tabasco sauce in case you needed to drown out the original flavour.

On my travels I often bumped into bored British service personnel. On one such pitstop I remember talking to a squaddie who complained she'd done little but look after a petrol pump for over six months. "I didn't sign up to the army to be a pump attendant." She was right, it didn't sound fun at all.

On the whole, the journey was thankfully uneventful. We reached the compound within the Green Zone and I was given a small room to myself. Despite the tiny size of the room, this was a definite privilege compared with the bunk rooms in which I could easily have found myself in.

As the capital city, Baghdad is suitably large and sprawling. We were based in the Green Zone, which had been completely taken over by the coalition forces. The river Tigris runs from north to south through the centre of Baghdad, meandering as it does so. A slow, ninety-degree turn creates a natural barrier on two sides and the Green Zone is located on the inside edge of the curve. While it offered some protection, it didn't entirely stop insurgents who would send mortars and other projectiles over the river. Our compound was sufficiently far away to be safe from such explosions, but they could still be heard quite easily.

I was chaperoned around Baghdad by a friendly guy called Charlie. He was kind enough to drive me around and I felt like a tourist being shown the sights by a native (although he clearly wasn't).

We went to the Victory Arch (also known as the Crossed Swords or more accurately the Swords of Qādisīyah), where I took some obligatory photos. The Victory Arch is where you've likely seen photos of Saddam Hussain inspecting his troops or from countless news reports. It's probably the most recognisable landmark in Iraq.

I must have been a bit blasé about the swords as the photos I have are quite bland; I couldn't even be bothered to have my photo taken standing in front of them and instead took my shot just leaning out of the car.

We also went to visit Saddam's Palace. I have no idea why places like this were open to visitors like me, just wandering around and taking a look. However, it was interesting so I'm not complaining. Charlie took me along to the gardens of the Palace to see the lions. Apparently Saddam wasn't beyond feeding them people occasionally, although that could easily be wishful thinking on the part of the rumourmongers.

We are so used to rigorous health and safety at places like safari parks, that it never crossed my mind that it wouldn't be completely safe to approach them. And yet, instead of a double fence with a safety gap between, the only thing separating me from the lions was a single chain-link fence. In fairness I was still quite safe, but it didn't feel that way for a moment when one of the lions took a run towards me and jumped up on the fence just a couple of metres away. Lions are very impressive when close up!

To remind people not to take advantage of the situation, there was a sign warning against feeding the lions 'live food such as dogs'. I'm not sure who was taking care of the lions, but they didn't look underfed. Hopefully they weren't full of dogs.

After only two or three days of IT jobs (and being a tourist), it was time to head back. I was due to travel back to Kuwait with a different team from the one I had travelled up with. This time the team leader seemed a little nervous and insisted on going over various possible eventualities with me before we set off. Pretty much every other team had just let me sit in the back with a promise that they'd handle anything that came up.

We set off, travelling through bustling Baghdad and onto the open road. After only about twenty or thirty minutes, the team lead got both vehicles to make a brief stop for a weapons check. This seemingly involved everyone (except me and the client, obviously) firing off a couple of rounds into the desert. It was probably a sensible precaution but at the time felt pointless and a little amateurish.

En route again and we covered a section of road where most of the tarmac was missing. The rough surface underneath kicked up incredible amounts of dirt when driven over and clouds were still present from previous vehicles. Despite that, the second vehicle kept in close proximity to the lead vehicle so as not to get separated. As I was in the second vehicle, I had the horrible experience of sitting in a car travelling at reasonable speed with a driver who was virtually blind.

Given that visibility was almost zero, this was achieved by the lead car communicating its speed for us to match. If we couldn't see, this must be good as we must still be just behind! If visibility improved it meant that we had dropped back too far, so we accelerated until we could see very little again. It was thoroughly terrifying for me and I was convinced we were going to rear-end the car in front at any second. It was probably only a minute or so before we hit smooth-ish tarmac again, but it seemed to last an age. It was probably the scariest part of the trip.

Although the team leader didn't entirely fill me with confidence, he was a really pleasant chap and ultimately, I can't fault his planning. On his list of things that could go wrong, was how to deal with a puncture. Having ascertained that I could change a wheel, he informed me that in the event of a flat, I would be in charge of sorting it out, leaving the client to stay safe and the protection team to do some protecting. It was the one and only time anyone planned with me what to do in this eventuality and the one and only time I ever got a puncture in the desert.

The 4x4s had a full-size spare on the boot which was easily accessible. It was quite a heavy vehicle which, when coupled with a rough, sandy road surface, made it quite tricky to jack up. Although the client had been asked to stay safe and out of the way, he couldn't help but get involved and I was thankful for that. The way he saw it, the safest course of action was to get us moving as quickly as possible. While he and I worked to change the wheel over to the spare, the rest of the team watched out for approaching hostiles.

The wheel change went smoothly and we were up and running again. You might be wondering what would happen if we had more punctures than spare wheels? In that situation or any other which rendered one vehicle un-driveable, the plan was the same. Abandon the broken vehicle and everyone cram into the remaining good vehicle. This was one of the reasons for always having a minimum two vehicle convoy, there would always be a second option. It might have been a bit of a squash but that would still beat walking home through the desert.

We crossed the border into Kuwait and arrived back at Kuwait City in the early evening. I was relieved to return to a safer location. Owing to increasing security concerns, I never went back to Baghdad, which was both a shame and a sensible decision.

CHAPTER THIRTEEN

Guns, danger and the realities of conflict

I may have managed to make it sound like all of this was just fun. Like a more adventurous version of Butlins but with more khaki than red coats. In reality, it was actually pretty dangerous. Not to start with but it certainly got that way.

In the immediate aftermath of the war, it was relatively peaceful. The locals seemed genuinely pleased to see the back of Saddam and were happy to receive support. Any minor violence was usually related to individuals looting or stealing. This may have been them taking advantage of the situation or a genuine need to survive in difficult circumstances.

As time crept on, most locals I spoke to were becoming increasingly frustrated with the continued foreign occupation, despite the 'help' being provided with reconstruction. Some help was useful, but it wasn't exactly asked for and I doubt there were any focus groups asking the locals whether they might prefer a new school and hospital over a power station. The Americans were spending their own money and chose to spend how they felt was best. They only saddled the Iraqis with the debt later.

It's also easy to malign companies like Olive as a bunch of

mercenaries seeking a fast dollar. Yes, they were there to make money, there's no doubting that. But as someone described to me early on, there's a distinct difference between a group of mercenaries and a security company. Security companies (proper ones anyway) seek to avoid danger whereas mercenaries go towards it (or even create the danger). Olive's role was one of protection and they were good at it. They didn't have the benefit of hindsight that would reveal the dubious reasoning behind starting the war or that it would drag on for so long and at the cost of so many lives. I, along with others at Olive, felt we were doing a genuine service and were aiming to improve the lives of the locals.

Olive team members worked hard to establish good links with locals and to help them where possible. It really did feel as though we were helping to rebuild a country, even if only in a small way. Flexing the scope of my IT fix-it credentials, I made several visits to the local bank to help them with various bits of kit, including a money counting machine. I didn't really know what I was doing, but I could competently dismantle it, clean it up and then put it back together. This seemed to improve matters, as did simply being there to help

I also helped a group of locals who were setting up an education facility to sort out their computers. None of this was in our official remit, but it was well received and I felt we were genuinely helping. I'm sure the cynical out there would claim it was only done to make our lives easier and I can understand that reasoning. But it didn't feel like it at the time. The military call actions like these 'winning over hearts and minds' and whatever the primary motivation, it's in everyone's interest to identify and then work towards mutual goals.

As time went on, hostilities towards foreign personnel increased, whether military, security company or civilian.

This limited contact with locals, which in turn further exacerbated poor relations. This was naturally disappointing and falling back to an 'us and them' attitude on both sides was never going to work well.

Interestingly, this always seemed the case with regards to relations between the locals and any Americans working in the area. When meeting a local for the first time, the initial question was often "British or American?", which would determine how I was then dealt with. It wasn't just locals taking exception to the Americans, sadly I witnessed poor behaviour on both sides. As the mainstay of the invading force, the Americans could have and should have done more to improve relations, at least in my opinion.

It's not just a case of Generals meeting with local Leaders, it has to happen at all levels. On one occasion, a group of us from Olive went to visit a team of locals helping to guard part of the port. We were chatting and sharing tea (which I drank only out of politeness; it was very sweet). An American Humvee[3] went past and when they spotted a group of figures huddled in the dark, they swung back to check us out. The Yanks got out and shone torches around. As soon as they saw that we were with the group, they visibly relaxed and came over to exchange a few words. Once they'd established we weren't a threat or any sort of problem, they got back in the vehicle and left. In that entire exchange, they didn't say one word to any of the locals, only to us. Politeness should have dictated at least a small greeting. After all, I was drinking tea that I didn't like for the benefit of good relations. They just didn't seem to know how to conduct themselves in order to foster better relations. As the dust and noise of their departure declined, the nearest Iraqi to me spat on the floor and said "Dirty Americans". He clearly wasn't impressed and

---

[3] A type of four-wheel-drive all-terrain military vehicle

neither was I. And all for sake of a simple hello.

Language doesn't have to be a barrier either, there are other ways of expressing friendship or even a joke. One team from Olive would often roll out their party trick at the port. They'd drive up to a group of locals with deliberate, pantomime scowls. The windows would be wound down, and as the locals looked over to see what the matter was, the team would jam the stereo on full blast playing a tape of local music they'd acquired from somewhere. The mood would instantly transform and everyone would start dancing, inside and outside the car. It never failed to generate smiles all round. Shared moments like that, however small, help to generate goodwill.

Unfortunately, Olive was just a tiny part of the picture. Although relations in the port were generally very good, elsewhere in Iraq things were continuing to decline. Looking back, it's easy to measure the increasing level of hostility by the cars and the driving tactics that were used.

To start with, when we simply needed cars in a hurry, we just got them from a car hire company at the airport. The lack of armour or other protection wasn't of concern. Technically, taking the hire cars over the border was a breach of the terms of the hire agreement, but no one worried about that. All the cars were at least chunky 4x4s, usually something like a Mitsubishi Pajero, but were otherwise perfectly standard.

They were less than a perfect standard by the time they were returned. As already mentioned, one of the agreed tactics in case of a problem with a vehicle was simply to abandon it. Even the ones that made it back to the hire car company were in a sorry state. They had been used and abused for many hundred miles through the desert. It would be fair to say that, other than ensuring they remained roadworthy, the teams didn't look after the cars very well at all. Inevitably they were returned in all sorts of messes, including some with bullet holes. I'm not sure whether Thrifty Hire Car were happy to accept this or not, given that they were hiring out a small fleet to us at a high day rate and could charge us exorbitant rates for any damage incurred.

Despite a complete lack of any training in defensive driving, I frequently drove around Iraq, although typically only for shorter distances. Indeed, some teams would insist on it, leaving everyone else in the vehicle (with suitable training) free to hold onto their guns. I also drove around Kuwait, across the desert and around the city. While this might not sound very exciting, road traffic accidents are the number one cause of death in many countries in the Middle East. You have to have your wits about you!

As time went on, we were able to get vehicles with some level of additional protection. Sadly this was increasingly a requirement, rather than a 'nice to have'. We started with vehicles that had been retrofitted with armour and moved onto vehicles built from the ground up with better protection. The retrofit ones were a pain. The additional armour of steel plates added a lot of weight, but the suspension and engine hadn't been upgraded to match. As a result they were slower to accelerate (or brake), but the real problem was when you hit a bump.

Bear in mind that Iraq at that time wasn't exactly smooth tarmac everywhere. Sections of road could be missing and huge pot holes were common place. The additional weight would drag the vehicle down heavily into any hole, but when the suspension caught up, it had a tendency to throw you upwards with such violence that banging your head on the ceiling was a real risk.

The doors were now much heavier, but again, the hinges hadn't been upgraded to match. When you got in and out, you had to close the door quickly. If you left it for too long, the door would sag on the hinges due to the excess weight and then you wouldn't be able to close it again.

In addition to the armour, we began to travel in convoy to all locations and regardless of the length of the journey. Initially this was just pairs, but soon became three vehicles as a minimum. On top of that, all occupants would be required to don body armour and a helmet. Each vehicle had a minimum of two security personnel, which meant that transporting a single client required a security team of at least six. It was like the world's most expensive taxi service. But probably not the most relaxing.

Within a period of about eighteen months we'd gone from me driving a regular hire car to a team of at least six, all well armed and driving in convoy in vehicles more akin to a tank than a car. It was a constant reminder of the increasing danger we were facing.

All of this effort wasn't just for show. In the period that I worked for Olive in Iraq, a total of eight members of the team were killed. Of those, two died in a road traffic accident (and arguably could have been saved with the presence of emergency services), two died in a gun battle with insurgents and four were blown up while travelling in vehicles by IEDs (two in Baghdad and two near Basra). This last loss of life via IED put an immediate stop to my trips into Iraq. From that moment on, all IT work was to be carried out by experienced military personnel only (even if they lacked the requisite IT experience). I would have to give support and advice remotely. While I was disappointed not to be able to continue to visit Iraq, I was relieved not to have to put myself into ever increasing danger. Inevitably there were further deaths for Olive staff.

That there could and likely would be deaths within the company was an understood risk. It was part of the job, just as it had been for everyone in their military careers. But that never reduced the great sadness when it occurred and the respect and reverence given to those who had lost their lives. Almost everyone arrived at Olive via recommendation, so they were often longstanding friends and colleagues. Each loss was felt keenly.

Unlike everyone else, I wasn't used to the idea of death being part of my day job. I was sad when it occurred but that didn't necessarily translate directly into fear for myself. You can't be (or at least I wasn't) scared all the time. Any apprehension I felt towards a particular task or journey soon dissipated and I soon found myself just getting on with things.

There were only three occasions when I felt real fear and in each case I wasn't actually in any real danger. The first came in Umm Qasr late one evening when the night suddenly erupted in gunfire. Everyone leapt up, starting to grab their weapons, body armour etc. Except me, obviously, who had nothing to do apart from stand around mutely and wonder if we were really under attack. We weren't. The Iraqi national football team were playing that night. They'd scored and the gunfire we heard was in celebration. I'm not sure how, but this information came in over the radio and we all had a good laugh.

The second 'oh-shit' moment also came in Umm Qasr. This time I was woken up early one morning by what sounded like massive explosions. I legged it out of my cabin to find out what was going on. Unexpectedly, the noise was coming from a really big game of conkers.

The giant metal shipping containers that lie around any port in the world are moved by massive cranes. The containers are secured from thievery by massive padlocks which are hard to remove without a lot of force. The crane operators would occasionally 'bump' the containers together in the hopes of knocking a padlock off. It's not very subtle and it's really, really loud. When the crane operators realised they'd been spotted the banging would stop. I thought we were being mortared or something.

The last big-fear moment is perhaps the oddest. After returning to Kuwait City from Baghdad, I went out for dinner with the rest of the crew the following evening. There was another team coming back that day, with whom I could have travelled instead, had I needed more time in Baghdad.

While in the restaurant we got a message to say the second team had arrived safely, but that they'd been shot at while on their way. The bullets had pierced the back of the vehicles and either safely passed through or been stuck in something harmless. In one case, the bullet had made it all the way through to the back of the driver's seat and had been stopped from travelling further by the driver's body armour.

At first we simply laughed it off, but it was only later that I realised that if I'd been travelling with them, they might have been picking the bullets out of me instead of the seat. I would almost certainly have been travelling in the rear seats, and the main area of protection in body armour isn't actually all that big.

It was a sobering thought and probably the most fear I felt throughout my whole experience. Despite the fact that nothing actually happened to me directly and at the time the fear hit I was quite safely dining in a restaurant.

Given that it was something I faced regularly, I often idly wondered what I would do in an actual crisis situation. My thoughts usually wandered from useful mental planning and into daydream territory. Sometimes I would consider what might happen if I was captured but often, in my head at least, I would grab a weapon from a fallen comrade and save the day. It was ridiculous to think I could do anything like that, but who daydreams about cowering in hole and then being shot in the stomach?

The attitudes towards me and guns varied quite a lot. Most

people were quite reasonably in the camp of 'he doesn't know what he's doing, don't let him near a gun'. I felt the same way but I was still tempted by the lure of them.

For a complete novice, holding a real gun in your hands can be a very powerful experience. Obviously they have the potential to do great harm, and holding this potential and having the power of it transferred to your control is a great force for the human mind. I can understand why people get hooked on this power; it is tempting to assert your control over the weapon by simply holding it and the feeling is addictive.

Once one of the Olive crew decided it would be sensible to equip me with a sidearm as a defensive measure. I didn't really agree, but despite myself, I was soon standing in front of Jim, our local team leader, listening while the case was made for me being armed. Thankfully Jim disagreed and I was denied a weapon.

"If we're under such hostile attack that the IT guy needs to be armed, we're all fucked anyway."

I sighed with relief because if I had been offered it, I probably would have said yes.

I was given a couple of opportunities to fire some guns though, and this only helped to reinforce the fact that I didn't really know what I was doing. The first time we went into the desert a short way and I was given a pistol to shoot at some empty drink cans. Gun in hand, I stood as I had seen in the movies, pointing towards the can that clearly deserved my wrath.

I hit it with my first shot! Clearly I was a natural.

Several more shots followed and I failed to hit it even once more. Perhaps this was harder than I thought.

The second time was slightly more formal. The various

groups (Army, RAF, Olive, etc.) in the port had set up a communal shooting range just outside the gates. This helped to avoid the kind of confusion which had been created by the celebratory gunfire for the Iraqi football team scoring, causing the whole port to go on alert. We couldn't stop the Iraqis from causing confusion, but we could at least prevent false alarms between each other. Plus it was a lot safer to have a dedicated space.

I was taken to the range and offered the chance to use an AK47. I actually felt more familiar with the AK than I had with the pistol. Back in the UK, a couple of friends in my village had air rifles. One of the benefits of spending part of my youth growing up in the Herefordshire countryside. We would take them out and fire at stationary objects like tree stumps. These we usually managed to hit but we would be a lot less successful shooting moving targets like rabbits or squirrels.

I was therefore quietly confident with the AK as I stepped forward onto the range, which is about where it all went wrong. I carefully lined up the far end of the barrel with my target, but only the tip, not along the length of the barrel. This is shooting 101 and the result of this basic error was that my shots were sailing several metres clear over the top of the target. After a few shots I did realise my error, brought the weapon level and successfully hit the target.

I thought about this a lot afterwards, and it goes to show the greatly increased pressure from using a real weapon when you don't know what you're doing. And why the military practise firing until it becomes second nature. Just the slightly increased pressure of a 'real' gun together with a small audience had caused me to miss terribly. It made me realise that in the confusion and pressure of an actual firefight, I doubted I'd get my act together enough to even fire the gun correctly, let alone in the right direction. My colleagues were right about not giving me a gun. It's harder than it looks.

One reasonable question to ask at this point is where all the guns came from. Initially, the guns were bought on the black market, although in Iraq it's probably just called the market. AK47s were the norm, and cost around $100, although the price went up a bit as demand increased. Smaller weapons like pistols were in much shorter supply and could cost more than $1000.

Given the origin of the guns, they weren't all in the best condition and varied quite a bit in quality. I naturally thought that all AK47s were from Russia, but that turned out to be a misconception. A lot of the weapons we had were manufactured in China. Regardless of their birthplace, they were all recognisably AK47s, although there was some variety in the style of the stock, handles and presumably, the quality.

Given the variability in the weapons, and the fact that each and every one might need to be relied on in a life-or-death situation, they had to be checked over, tested and fixed. After a while, Olive had so many guns that they flew a weapons specialist over from British Columbia to give them all a thorough going over. I was fortunate enough to witness this artist at work, although the nuances of what he was doing were largely lost on me. I did enjoy watching all the serious old-hands who in turn were watching this specialist work his magic. They were enthralled as the guy quickly stripped gun after gun, rebuilding and approving some while rejecting others. The rejected parts were rebuilt to make newly working units with surprisingly little scrap by the time he'd finished.

As time went by, more modern looking weapons were obtained through more official channels. I was shown things like MP5 machine guns, which were shorter than most of the

AKs. One former marine called Simon spent an evening showing me how the MP5 worked and a few routines for handling it. It was fascinating but I'm sorry to say I can't remember a thing about it now. With a bit of luck, it won't matter that I still don't know how to handle a machine gun.

CHAPTER FOURTEEN

The Bear Pit

Once enough wrecks had been lifted from the seabed of the port of Umm Qasr, ships could start coming in and out and the goods could start flowing. Once that happened, things got a lot busier. The constant flow of people changed the security situation and a lot more effort had to be dedicated to the running of the port and not just protecting it.

There were now a lot more Gurkhas helping to man checkpoints, supplemented by and working alongside some local Iraqis. The increased number of people and activity gave the place a real buzz which I enjoyed witnessing and occasionally getting involved in.

Right next door to our warehouse, on the other side of the shipping container wall, was the Bear Pit. At times as intimidating as the name suggests, the Bear Pit was orchestrated mayhem.

I still don't have a great deal of experience working in a port, but I'm pretty confident that in most major ports around the world, things are planned out well in advance. For any given shipment arriving to be unloaded, its onward progression will be mapped out to the letter. A company will be enlisted to collect and shift the goods, a driver will be chosen to show up in a given vehicle and so on. Not at Umm Qasr.

The principle was similar, but the organisation was a lot more last-minute and hectic. The goods would show up on a boat and the owner/purchaser or some other representative would arrive at the port with the appropriate paperwork to claim the delivery. At this point they would have a slip of paperwork authorising the collection of the goods, a giant shipping container to unload and not much else.

Negotiations would occur with two groups in order to get things moving. First, a driver and vehicle would be chosen. A huge line of brightly painted and adorned lorries would form a line outside the port waiting for business. The drivers would hide under their vehicles to avoid the bright sunshine or sit alongside them drinking tea when it was cool enough for them to do so. The owner of the goods would go along the line to find and negotiate with a driver for transportation. Once done, they would bring the driver and his lorry into the port area, allowing them through.

At this point there would be two or three individuals involved but, in most cases, this wasn't nearly enough to quickly unload the container onto the lorry. So, the owner would negotiate with a second group, a local team or, more appropriately, gang of lads, to help shift the kit. In an ideal world, the gang would quickly, efficiently and carefully unload the goods from the container onto the lorry.

In reality, how smoothly this went would depend on how much the owner had paid the gang. Or more accurately, whether the gang felt they had been paid enough. If they felt they'd been underpaid (yet had presumably accepted the job anyway to avoid a day without pay), they would usually attempt to make up their shortfall by stealing whatever it was they were helping to shift. Loads were frequently electronic goods, which could range from small radios to large air conditioning units. Obviously, some items were easier to steal than others. The owner would therefore march around while the work was done to oversee and police his own workforce.

Where things really got exciting was when the owner tipped his gang extra to go and steal stuff from other containers that were also being unloaded. When he wasn't keeping an eye on his own gang, he'd look at what else was being unloaded and then go back to his own gang with a shopping list of things to grab. A well-paid gang would defend the goods that they were unloading whereas an underpaid gang would turn a blind eye. Or possibly even assist.

This all happened in an area that was meant to be cordoned off, probably the size of a couple of football pitches. While this might sound quite large, it didn't feel spacious when occupied by cars, lorries, mountains of boxes and a couple of hundred busy, frantic Iraqis. It was wonderful to watch the chaos and simple busy-ness of it all.

Most of the time the Bear Pit was simply full of the routine motion of unloading and loading. Occasionally the mass of movement would shift as something sparked a change. I would see someone grab a box and make a dash, either to escape directly or to throw their stolen goods over a wall to someone waiting on the other side. They would then try to climb over themselves or try to find a different escape route.

Olive's official role in all this was only supervisory. We weren't really meant to get involved, but should simply drive around the Bear Pit, creating an overt presence. It was impossible not to get involved though and the team would chase down would-be thieves, returning them and their swag to the thankful owner.

Clearly, I didn't have a lot to contribute here, but I enjoyed sitting in the back of the patrol 4x4, keeping an eye out for that moment of excitement. After all, if none of the computers needed fixing, I might as well stay occupied!

Throughout this book, I have so far referred to the port as a single location. But it was actually two ports next to each other, not very creatively called the old port and the new port. The new port was the one we were at and apparently the one that needed our primary attention. The old port was still very active, although it was only accessible to much smaller shipping vessels. The security in the old port was run entirely by local Iraqis, but we provided assistance and support whenever we could.

A lot of the goods unloaded at the old port were foodstuffs, so in some ways, it was actually more of a target for looting. I remember listening in to negotiations with one of the local security teams. They had managed to recover half a dozen bags of grain from looters and wanted to keep one for themselves rather than return them all. Given how little they were paid, it was hard to deny them some food, even though it wasn't really ours to give.

When looters were caught, they were often handed over to the Olive team for us to deal with. We weren't judge, jury and executioner though, and it would hardly have curried favour with the locals if we were doling out rough justice. Usually the caught looters were locked in a shipping container for a few hours before being let out again.

Like the Bear Pit, I had no qualification or indeed excuse for being at the old port, but it was interesting to get involved with the various people and help out where I could. Mostly I simply observed and enjoyed the thrill of it all.

Other countries

CHAPTER FIFTEEN

Kuwait

Olive outgrew their first office in Kuwait pretty quickly and we relocated to a larger one. This was actually four flats taking up an entire floor in an apartment block. It was quite an enterprise, with some staff permanently located there and many others passing through on their way to or from projects in Iraq. There were sufficient people typically for it to be worth employing a full-time, in-house cook.

The food was usually very good, but we still found time to eat out now again. I enjoy eating local cuisine while abroad, but it's actually very hard to do so in Kuwait, as well as nearly everywhere else I went to in the Middle East. That's not to say it's hard to eat out, just that it's hard to eat local food. Food outlets were almost entirely international fast-food joints or restaurant chains such as McDonalds, Wendy's and TGI Fridays. As a dry country in terms of alcohol, there are no pubs or clubs to go to. To a degree, eating out seemed to have replaced going to the pub from a social perspective. This was less true for the younger generations who seemed instead to roam around the enormous shopping malls. In lieu of other social environments in which to interact with their peers, they would dress up to the nines and generally loiter about, seemingly without purpose.

Although Kuwait was officially dry and the punishments for having or consuming alcohol were quite severe, it was still possible to get booze. I went out for dinner with Lee and Simon to a small Chinese restaurant that Lee had found. We had a great meal which we managed to drag out so long that we were the last ones in the restaurant. When the waitress came to take our plates away, she asked if we had enjoyed our meal. We said truthfully that we had, but perhaps a little more enthusiastically than we needed to. "Great", she said, "I'll get the chef out so you can tell her yourself".

Moments later the chef appeared. She was keen to chat, asked about our meal and then where we were from. I struggled to understand her thick accent, but regardless, it was apparent that she was pretty drunk. The happy sort of drunk rather than the falling over sort.

We asked in a knowing fashion whether or not there was anywhere nearby to go and get a drink. With a wicked grin and a tap to the side of her nose, she disappeared back into the kitchen. She reappeared moments later armed with four shot glasses. These were passed around, including another for herself. From her chatter we realised that this was her own brew which she made on the premises. If she disclosed exactly what it was made from, I failed to pick that up.

Cheered by our discovery we all tried the concoction and then each tried to cover up the fact that it was horrendous. It was extremely harsh to drink but we all managed it and then tried to tell our host how great it was. Thankfully she didn't go and get us any more.

Booze wasn't the only time I found myself on the wrong side of religious customs. On more than one occasion I managed to time my trip to Kuwait with Ramadan. During this month-long celebration, Muslims are required to observe fasting during daylight hours. Given that Kuwait is a Muslim majority country, restaurants close during the day to all customers, regardless of faith. While out and about I forgot this until my stomach rumblings reminded me that getting lunch was going to be tricky. Once, I managed to forget completely until I crashed into the closed doors of a McDonalds.

While I do my best to observe and respect local customs, I also find it hard to skip mealtimes entirely! Out of desperation, I ended up in a supermarket where we found we could buy sandwiches. We had to take them into the car park where we tried to eat them as discreetly as possible, ducking down below the level of the dashboard to take furtive bites. I felt guilty for doing so, but also laughing at myself for being in the situation with my illegal sandwich.

Larger supermarkets often had an electronics department. They would sell the usual TVs, stereos and so on. Sometimes they would have a dedicated counter selling games consoles. You could choose to buy your console with or without a chip added, allowing it to bypass certain security checks and to play pirated games. They then had a folder of pirate games for you to choose from, as well as original copies. Copied pirate films were also on offer. I'm not sure if this was illegal in Kuwait but it certainly would have been in the UK. Not what you would expect to find in the equivalent of Sainsbury's.

While it's easy to be relaxed about local rules and customs, particularly when you're casually circumventing them, it's always worth bearing in mind the penalties for breaking the law. While western ex-pats were often given a little leeway, that wasn't the case for everyone and certainly couldn't be relied upon. While there, we saw an article in a local newspaper giving notice of a public execution for the smuggling and distribution of alcohol. Penalties could be extremely harsh and the authorities weren't against using you as a warning and example if it suited their needs.

During one particularly lengthy trip, I realised I could do with a haircut. One of the other chaps was going and I went along with him to a barber he had visited before. As well as the haircut, I was talked into having a shave with a cut-throat razor. I'd never been shaved by anyone else at that point, and certainly not by someone brandishing anything as terrifying as a cut-throat. I told myself it would be a good experience so I sat there feeling nervous and looking forward to when it was over.

First, I had a hot towel wrapped around my face. It was excruciatingly hot and I would have liked to howl but nerves and general Britishness overcame me and I endured my pain in silence. When the barber then came at me for the shave, I was both slightly disappointed and greatly relieved to see he had a regular Gillette razor! I've still yet to tick this particular experience off my list, but I'm okay with that.

CHAPTER SIXTEEN

Jordan and Qatar

Olive offices began to spring up in other locations and I started to venture further afield. One guy was visiting the Kuwait office but was normally based in Amman, Jordan. He said he'd really appreciate it if I came over to sort out a few issues and I happily agreed. From his description, I reckoned it could be done in a few hours, so I said I'd just come over for one night.

"You should make a few days out of it", he said, "It's five stars!".

No Olive office had yet been described as five stars, so I ignored his suggestion and arranged flights for a measly 24 hours in Jordan. To this day, I'm not sure why I did that. Even if it had been a bit crap, it still would have been interesting to explore a little. As it turns out, it was far from a bit crap.

I don't know why, perhaps simple expediency, but, unusually, we had taken up office space and accommodation in the very much five-star Intercontinental Hotel in Amman. It was glorious and I realised the mistake of my short duration trip as soon as I arrived. The team there definitely living the high life with luxurious accommodation and taking time out by the pool each lunchtime.

Unfortunately, as I'd only given myself 24 hours, I couldn't even join them at the pool for my one lunchtime as I had to get all the work done. The guy who'd originally invited me over was chuckling at my flawed decision. He did generously offer to invent some massive IT failure so I could stay on a couple of days. I should have taken him up on the offer but I was either too honest or too scared of being discovered. A common complaint on any business trip is that you don't get to see much other than airports and hotels. On this occasion, that would have been just fine.

I ended up doing exactly the same thing when visiting Doha in Qatar about a year later, although this time it was my own schedule that limited me to just one night. Again, Olive had acquired office space in the local Intercontinental and it was equally plush. Somehow, I had missed out on the luxury of a longer stay for a second time.

I wish I could comment on both Qatar and Jordan as countries but sadly I wasn't there long enough to gain an impression. What little I saw was similar to the rest of the Middle East I had already visited at that point.

CHAPTER SEVENTEEN

Saudi

Olive's two other main locations in the Middle East became Riyadh in Saudi Arabia and Dubai in the United Arab Emirates. To me, they show different ends of the regional spectrum.

My first trip to Saudi demonstrated its oddness and position as one of the more severe countries in the Middle East. By this time, I would place myself as a fairly accomplished flyer. I had long since ditched the tan suit in favour of jeans and a t-shirt or whatever was comfortable. Still, despite being a more confident traveller, my arrival in Saudi made me feel slightly uncomfortable. As soon as I landed I was targeted by the customs guards. I'm confident this was less to do with my lack of suit jacket and more the fact that I was the only westerner on the flight. I was clearly the only person of interest to them.

They went through my bags and found a wallet full of DVDs. They insisted on going through, point at each in turn and repeating the same question.

"Is this a blue movie?"
"No" to 'Austin Powers'

"No" to 'Platoon'
"No", "No", "No"

I'm sure that they recognised all of the films as we went through them, they just wanted to put a bit of pressure on me. After they'd finished examining my questionable movie collection, I was free to go.

Despite the interruption, I still had a few hours to kill before my internal connecting flight to Riyadh. Large airports are almost always 24-hour affairs. Regardless of the time of day, you can usually waste masses of time browsing around shops and restaurants, should you feel the need. With this in mind, I set off to look around the airport and to waste some time before my next flight.

I was surprised to find that large swathes of the place were closed with most of the lights turned off. None of it had been cordoned off, and I was seemingly free to roam in semi-darkness around the many halls and corridors. It was spooky, and at times I felt as if I had wandered through the wrong door into an area where I shouldn't be. I wasn't the only one, although that was almost true. A few other curious or bored souls were also wandering around, peering through the dimness into even darker shop windows. It didn't exactly make the place feel friendly or welcoming. Nothing bad happened to me there, but I felt very uncomfortable and nervous that if something untoward did occur, I would be completely out of my depth to handle it.

On arrival at my final destination, I was met at the airport by someone from Olive. We drove through Jeddah with the usual mix of desert interspersed with the likes of Starbucks. Olive was based on-site with a client, this time one of the oil giants.

This took the form of a large and well-established compound. It was protected on all sides by high white walls.

The single entrance in and out had a traffic-slowing chicane made of large concrete blocks. I wasn't surprised to see armed guards, but I wasn't expecting the large, fixed-placement machine gun. It looked as though they were preparing for a full-on assault.

Despite the hostile arrival, once inside the compound it felt more like a holiday village. There were little cul-de-sacs of houses around a central hub. The hub contained a sports centre and a generously sized outdoor swimming pool next to a bar and restaurant. Rather than cook, the Olive team based there would eat the majority of their meals by the pool. Not a bad life!

The holiday village feeling dissipated a little the next day. The house that the Olive team were in was having the windows upgraded to ones with bullet proof glass. While this might sound a bit over the top, within the next couple of years there were several attacks on similar compounds. I was asked to keep an eye on the installation team while the Olive crew popped out.

"Keep checking on them otherwise they'll be asleep on the job", I was told.

I assumed this statement wasn't to be taken literally, but it was. When I dutifully popped upstairs to see how things were going, a number of the workers had laid out cardboard on the floor and were busy trying to take a nap. On seeing me, they begrudgingly started to get up again, but clearly had no shame in being caught.

One other interesting behaviour was a kind of fatalism towards meetings. Some of the Olive team were trying hard to drum up new business in the area. A local Saudi group had been delayed by traffic on the way to a meeting with the Olive team. Apparently, the snarl up had been enough to convince them that the meeting wasn't meant to be. They turned around and went back, missing the meeting altogether. And then refused to rearrange anything. The Olive team weren't used to doing business this way and were quite frustrated.

While out on a trip to pick up equipment, one chap explained things to me as he saw it. While sitting in a ubiquitous Starbucks, he had apparently witnessed one lady whipped in the car park outside the coffee shop. The so-called 'religious police' had decided to administer swift justice due to her inappropriate dress.

"This place tricks you into thinking it's all normal, and then something like that happens".

From my brief visits, Saudi certainly felt less welcoming than other Gulf states I had the opportunity to go to. We certainly only left the compound when necessary, so opportunities to explore were greatly diminished.

Entertainment was limited to within the compound. We spent one evening having a movie night using a projector to create a giant picture up onto the wall. I don't remember the movie, but it was some sort of romcom and the whole room was quiet while we watched together. How romantic!

On the subject of television, I would like to point out the dedication with which most of the team watched a show called 'Ultimate Force' while it was on. A fictional show about the SAS but co-written by genuine ex-SAS soldier and later author, Chris Ryan; it starred Ross Kemp. I would routinely hear complaints about how unrealistic it was or derision about some factual aspect or other. It was generally referred to rather ungenerously as 'Ultimate Farce'. Others would join in, commenting or simply nodding sagely about the obvious faults. But the fact remained – they all watched it! Just like real spies probably enjoy watching James Bond, the escapism can still be fun, even if you know more than most about how silly it is.

CHAPTER EIGHTEEN
United Arab Emirates

I've noted that a few locations I visited had a slight holiday feel about them, but Dubai really is a holiday destination. As Olive set up an office there, I was lucky enough to visit a couple of times. It's an extraordinary place and quite different when compared with the rest of the Gulf area.

In the early 2000s, the United Arab Emirates were trying to attract international businesses to set up offices by creating special zones. These zones were limited to the sort of businesses they wanted moving in and these were offered tax incentives to do so. Olive's first office was placed in one such zone.

Unusually, it was actually just an office and looked a lot smarter than other Olive locations, even during the evenings. That was probably because it wasn't also used as a hotel. By now Olive was getting quite a bit larger, probably over a hundred people, so there was a variety of accommodation. Some staff had their own permanent locations and there was a nice villa that some of the senior staff shared on a semi-permanent basis. And, of course, there was a slightly less plush but quite large flat for those like me who were typically visiting for short periods.

The flat was fine but not particularly special. It was in a great location though, just walking distance from a couple of Dubai's most prominent landmarks of the time. These days, Dubai is awash with prominent landmarks.

The Burj Al Arab (advertised as the world's first seven-star hotel) was within easy viewing distance, an impressive sight. It remained a sight only, sadly, as it was apparently quite a task to get in. The Souk Madinat was just next door, also impressive and with a much more relaxed door policy. The Souk is supposed to represent an old Arabian market but it's too air-conditioned and clean to be a very accurate reflection. Well stocked with shops and restaurants, it's still a very pleasant experience though, and has far more character than your average shopping centre. Outside are more restaurants lining artificial but attractive waterways fed with water drawn from the sea alongside. A perfect postcard picture experience, you can even take to a gondola if you so desire.

Dubai has quite a reputation as a party city and it's fairly well earned. Compared with pretty much any other city in the region, alcohol is fairly easy to get hold of. There are bars and even nightclubs to enjoy. We tried a nightclub called Cyclones which had a good reputation but also a seedier side. Walking in, the first section we strolled through was quite a sight. It seemed entirely populated by Russian looking women draped over Arab men. Further back was more my style, a cheesy disco that wouldn't have been out of place in any student bar in the UK.

Seemingly, a lot of the Arab men in such places weren't even locals, at least not local to Dubai. On one flight there from Saudi, the aeroplane was packed with men I was sagely informed later were heading over for the weekend "to do all the things they can't do back in their own country".

It's not all fun and giggles though. Most people will have seen in the news what happens when things go wrong for unwary visitors expecting a no-holds barred party. Visiting Brits have ended up on the wrong side of the law by drinking in the wrong place or even getting frisky in a public place like one of the many beaches. Dubai is certainly more relaxed than most other places in the Middle East, but it's still possible to end up in serious trouble.

This seems an appropriate place to discuss the situation with labour in the Middle East. This is by no means exclusive to the United Arab Emirates, but they've had more bad press about it than other countries, with workers dying in droves on internationally recognised projects. Foreign labour is invited over to work from countries such as India, Sri Lanka and Bangladesh (among others). While pay might be better than in their home country, working conditions are typically fairly poor and for many it's pretty close to or actually lethal. Workers never gain the full rights enjoyed by a local and can be thrown out at a moment's notice. The arrangement is precarious but apparently not poor enough to put off the next tranche from setting off to try their luck.

Most countries in the Middle East are propped up by such a workforce, which isn't too far off slave labour. Pretty much all menial work seems to be done by such workers and fleets of them can be seen on any building project, roadworks or simply cleaning up around you. Regardless of the time of day or scorching temperatures, they are still present. It's hard not to feel sorry for them and I can't see that the problem will be resolved in a hurry. As long as foreign workers continue to be tempted overseas by the promise of higher wages, the Middle East will welcome them to do their dirty work.

The one interesting exception to this was Iraq. Its borders were virtually closed for so long that importing labour was never an option. I discussed this with a native Iraqi one day and he claimed it was a good thing and made the Iraqi nation and its people 'tougher'.

CHAPTER NINETEEN
Growing pains

I think it would be fair to say that Olive found success out in the Middle East. They continued to win new contracts and take on new staff. Like any business that's busy growing, cash flow can become a problem. Sending whole teams of people out to the desert cost the company wages, flights, accommodation, vehicles and so on.

The founders needed cash to fund their growth and turned to two very well-off brothers, Charles and Danny. Between them they invested money into the business to help with the cashflow and allow it to grow as quickly as clients were bringing new contracts.

Danny was rarely seen but Charles began working in the office in London soon afterwards. It would be fair to say that I had a difficult relationship with Charles. Whereas everyone else until that point had treated me as an equal, I felt Charles treated me very much as an underling.

He would ask me to show him how to do something on the computer and if it approached anything remotely close to tricky (or just boring), he would quickly give up and instruct me to do it for him. This extended to other things as well, including once asking me to clean the dust off the screen of his mobile phone.

This could have been more tolerable, but he was also the most inept at using a computer and I would have to sort out some problem or other for him at least once a week. Or it felt like that anyway. If I wasn't in the office, he would chase me down on the phone instead.

There seemed no escape, even the supposed sanctity of the weekends offered no protection. I received a phone call from him one Sunday while at a family event in Cheltenham. Having explained that I would need to return to the office to fix something on the server to complete his request, he asked me when that would be. I told Charles that I wouldn't be back in London until that evening and I could go straight to the office if necessary. He told me it was necessary and then he proceeded to phone me hourly to ask if I'd left yet. After travelling into the office on my Sunday evening, I eventually resolved the issue. I received the scantest of thanks for my trouble. I don't mind the occasional disturbance to my personal life, but with Charles it seemed routine and something that didn't trouble him to do in the slightest.

I wasn't the only one who struggled with Charles although I was never privy to the details. Unfortunately, Johnny, one of the original founders, also fell out with Charles to the point that he felt obliged to leave the company altogether. This was a real blow to the business and to me personally. I had a lot of respect for Johnny and of the two, I knew whom I would rather have stayed.

Of the other founders, Dougie took a backseat to the point where it looked a lot more like retirement than anything else. JY stayed on, but spent so much time in Iraq that he can't have had a lot do with the running of the business, although I could be doing both of them a disservice.

Despite this watering down of the original founders, the business continued to go from strength to strength. Within two years or so of my joining, the company had grown to around 450 staff and contractors. We moved from Mayfair to a larger office near Hyde Park Corner and of course opened various offices overseas.

This success was evident by our increasingly extravagant Christmas parties. While they weren't on a par with the excesses that London finance is known for, they were still pretty good, particularly compared with what I'd been used to back in Hereford.

One year we went to a Japanese seafood restaurant on Park Lane. The now-disgraced Sir Philip Green was sitting at the next table flanked by a couple of models. I've no idea what I had to eat that night, but it was definitely fantastic.

The next year we went to the Groucho Club, an apparently well-known landmark that I had no knowledge of. The highlight of that evening was a raffle, the top prize was a week in Dubai with all expenses paid and an extra five days holiday with which to enjoy it. I'm very confident the raffle was rigged, as all the prizes went to very deserving people. The top one went to Theresa, our incredibly hard-working office manager. She had the unenviable task of arranging flights and travel for an ever-growing workforce that couldn't sit still in one place for very long. I won a champagne trip for two on the London Eye, so I'm not complaining.

CHAPTER TWENTY

Interviewing others.

Finding that many new people for the security teams wasn't very easy. Despite what a trip to any pub in Hereford might suggest, there aren't actually that many ex-SAS men sitting around waiting for employment. The chaps within Olive quickly exhausted their personal contacts list and had brought in almost everyone that was readily available. On top of that, there were now many other security companies also vying for anyone still looking for a job.

But working as a security professional in Iraq isn't really something you can learn on the job. People have to be suitably trained and Olive began putting together a list of acceptable qualifications. Their criteria were that individuals had to have served at least two tours in hostile environments and passed a suitable course in close protection. They even had a list of where and when qualified as suitably hostile. The tour aspect would obviously have to be done while still serving in the military, but the course could be completed afterwards if necessary.

There were a number of companies providing close protection training and they attracted a steady stream of ex-military and non ex-special forces personnel willing to sign up. Olive wasn't the only company that would turn up on graduation day to try to scoop up the best candidates as they left the podium.

Given that they'd widened the net, Olive became a melting pot for a wider mix of people of various backgrounds and places. As well as British Army veterans, we took on former Marines, and guys originally from units in Australia, South Africa and elsewhere. I enjoyed talking to all these new people and learning a bit more about their parts of the world. I was also faced with learning even more lingo.

"I'm just going for a swamp and then we'll grab a wet".

This just sounded like nonsense to me the first time I heard it, but translated to;

"I'm just going to the toilet and then we'll grab a cup of tea".

I was beginning to need a dictionary.

This additional recruitment was helping but on occasions we would still try other avenues. Once Olive tried an open day at the London office in an effort to attract more people. Despite the advert clearly stipulating the minimum criteria, it didn't stop forty or so very unsuitable people turning up to try their luck. Apparently, the fabled riches of the Middle East were attractive enough to overcome peoples' fear of getting shot.

One chap felt his experience as a postman qualified him to carry a gun while protecting himself and others from hostiles. Another guy was so old that the interviewer felt obliged to question his fitness and suitability for 'running through the desert while carrying heavy equipment and body armour'.

"I'm not that old", he replied, "I've still got all my own teeth".

While the interviewer felt that it was commendable that he still had a full smile, it wasn't really enough to qualify him for close protection work.

Despite these obvious and foolhardy attempts to fake their way to the desert, these individuals were always easy to spot, until one candidate almost managed it. Unlike all the others, he spoke the lingo and seemed to come with the right background and qualifications. He was added to the list of accepted candidates and work began to sort out his visas and travel plan. That is, until a routine background check showed he'd been making it all up.

His interviewers were really surprised that he had managed to fool them as he'd been so convincing. The lingo had apparently come straight from reading books like Bravo Two-Zero and he was, in reality, a baggage handler at Manchester airport. I wonder how long he thought he would be able to fake it? Right up to the point that people were shooting at him perhaps.

There were others that met the criteria but were still unsuitable. They were sometimes harder to weed out. Two guys made it all the way to a project in Basra and were ready to start. The night before they went out the first time, they got drunk and ended up in a fight. They were shipped straight back without hesitation. In a world where a lack of professional standards could result in multiple deaths, the company didn't take chances.

CHAPTER TWENTY-ONE

IT pains

As the company grew past 400 in number, running all the IT was becoming an epic task. I've worked for similar sized companies since, and they typically have an IT department of around a dozen people. Olive continued to have just me.

I was responsible for all the IT in all the countries we had offices, which covered London and half of the Middle East. Plus anywhere else a team happened to be at any given time. Over the course of time, I dealt with support calls from North America, Europe, Africa and the Far East.

That meant firewalls, networking kit, servers, laptops and anything else that could go wrong. Including, on occasions, the overly-complicated coffee machine in our London office. If it had a battery or plug, it became the responsibility of the IT department, which meant me.

If the email went down, it wasn't just 'a bit of a problem', it was very heavily relied upon for a lot of our communications. Cloud-based services didn't really exist and our email was run from a server in the basement in London. And that server had to keep running because there were no other options that could be relied upon to keep the whole company talking.

There was no country-wide mobile phone network in Iraq.

There was a small network in Baghdad which had limited coverage and you could also pick up a signal if you were near to the Kuwaiti border, but that was about it. That meant that for teams to communicate with each other and to find out which roads were safe to travel, they relied on email. They could generally get onto the internet at any coalition facility, which were dotted around, or use a portable satellite-based setup. Although not all teams had the satellite gear as it was expensive to buy and eye-wateringly expensive to use. No option was great, but that was all that was available. And if they signed in to get emailed updates and found the email was down, that could lead to a serious problem.

I was, perhaps, a victim of my own success. Despite the strains on both the equipment and myself, I was in general managing to keep things afloat. Given the reliance on email and IT, Olive ought to have been showering me with a large budget. Instead they adopted the attitude that if it works now, then there's no need to spend more.

I had put in requests to purchase things that would seem now to be fundamental, such as a large UPS[4] to keep the main servers running in the event of a power-cut, a tape backup system and air-conditioning for the small space we optimistically called the server room.

With no-one on the board representing or taking responsibility for the IT (and me not being senior enough for a place on the board), every request was declined. There was money for lots of other things, but IT apparently didn't warrant it.

And then the situation changed quite radically.

Olive took on a new member of staff, a really nice bloke called Damian. His background was IT, not military and amongst other things, he was to be my new boss. He also sat

---

[4] Uninterruptible Power Supply, also known as a battery.

on the senior meetings and took responsibility for IT as a whole. Finally, I had a voice.

It would be fair to say that I didn't impress him to start with. He asked about the IT and I told him honestly how bad a state things were in and how it was all just hanging together with sticky tape. I think he thought I was completely irresponsible.

Damian asked what I'd done to remedy the long list and I showed him all the planning I'd done, together with the purchase requests that had all been declined. From what I understand, he then told anyone that would listen that the whole thing was two steps from disaster and the only things keeping that from happening were luck and my hard work. Damian was my new best friend!

Everything I had been asking for was green-lit at once and I spent the next six months sorting it all out. I was still chronically busy, but at least it felt like progress instead of constant fire-fighting.

CHAPTER TWENTY-TWO

Moving on

Most of the security teams worked on deployment seven days a week for six weeks and then had three weeks off. They continued on this rotation indefinitely. Others based in offices in London or elsewhere would work a more regular routine. I had the worst of both worlds as I would work seven days a week while deployed but then come back to London to return to a Mon-Fri routine.

On top of that, I would be on the phone taking calls from anywhere and at any time, particularly as the working week is different in the Middle East. Even on holiday there was no escape as there was no one else for them to call. I was the entirety of the IT department. Although I was frustrated by the situation, I don't think I realised at the time how close to burning out I must have been.

In hindsight I should have spoken to someone about it before it became overwhelming, but instead I sat on the problem.

Change then came knocking once again. I was approached by John, the same guy that had introduced me to Olive in the first place. He had another opportunity for me through a friend of his, and would I be interested? More about that in the next chapter, but suffice to say that I accepted.

I handed my notice in with Olive, which was a mixed bag. Damian was helpful and asked me my reasons for leaving. I duly gave them, and very quickly I was offered a reasonable solution to everything. If I stayed, I would get a pay rise, time off in lieu (to reflect additional time worked while away) and most importantly, someone else to join the team so I could go on holiday without interruption. In fairness to Olive, it was everything I had asked for, but I am, apparently, quite stubborn and so I stuck to my decision.

At the beginning of my three-month notice period, things didn't go as I expected. Because what happened was precisely nothing at all. There was no move to replace me and everyone else behaved as though I wasn't really leaving. After almost a month of nothing, I approached Simon, our Head of Recruitment and pointed out that if they didn't find someone fast, they would be without anyone running the IT, which could be a problem. Plus, whoever did arrive after me would almost certainly struggle without some sort of handover. Picking up someone else's network is tricky, and documentation only goes so far.

"Good point", said Simon and went off to have a word with someone in the senior leadership team. Moments later they approached me and said something that still rates as one of the most insulting things anyone has ever said to me.

"Graeme"
"Yes"
"You're leaving"
"Yes"
"Do we"… (long pause) … "Do we need to replace you?"

I couldn't believe that they thought that the company might be able to manage without anyone running their IT.

What did they think I did with my time? Perhaps emboldened by my planned departure, I quipped back:

"You wouldn't manage more than a week without me, let alone the rest of the company".

"Hmmm", he responded, "Good point".

He turned on his heels and walked off. And with that meagre recognition that I might have added some value to the company after all, the search for my replacement had begun.

CHAPTER TWENTY-THREE

Interviewer

The next two months became one of my most enjoyable periods at Olive. The pressure was off a little and I started to help Simon find a suitable replacement. The first thing we had to do was decide what my job title should be. I hadn't had anything official until then, but we needed something to put on the job advert. I was immediately christened 'Global IT Manager' which sounded glamorous. If only I'd ever had business cards with that written on it.

The job adverts went out and the interviews began. We had quite a few candidates apply and almost all had the right IT skills. It wasn't simply about driving a keyboard though. Simon was keen to find someone that would fit from a personality point of view, together with a strong work ethic and flexibility to be shunted around countries like I had been.

When interviewing the candidates, Simon didn't pull his punches and deliberately made me sound quite heroic in order to gauge their reaction. Phrases like 'weeks away from home' and 'short notice flights to the Middle East' certainly put one or two off. And Simon always said the same thing when we'd reached that point;

"If that would put you off, no problem, there's the door".

No one ever took up the offer to leave halfway through, but I definitely saw some bottoms lift off the chair a bit. One poor chap asked what sort of work he might be expected to do in Iraq. Without a flicker of mirth to give himself away, Simon responded;

"As a small company, we all have to be pretty flexible. Only last week Graeme had to parachute into Fallujah to lead a hostage negotiation".

The poor candidate looked horrified and even when Simon assured him that it was a joke, he still didn't look convinced. If he'd have been looking towards me instead of Simon, he'd have seen I wasn't doing nearly as well at keeping a straight face. It was cruel, it was hilarious but it was also justified. Working with a lot of ex-squaddies in quite high-pressure environments wasn't for the faint hearted. A certain willingness for adventure, together with a very robust sense of humour, were definite requirements.

CHAPTER TWENTY-FOUR

Ozzie time

Time to find a replacement for me was beginning to run out, but then Olive got lucky. An Australian chap called Hayden came in for interview and fit the bill exactly. Fortunately, he was only on a one-month notice period which meant by the time he reached Olive, we would still have a three-week handover before I finally left. Hayden was offered the role, and much to my relief, accepted.

When Hayden started, we planned out how to spend the available time for completing the handover. Of the three weeks, we planned to spend almost two weeks of it travelling and visiting various Olive locations. It was a great trip. With Hayden just getting started and me just on my way out, it was pretty relaxing. I introduced Hayden to the main figures at each office, along with showing him the kit, where it was located and how it was wired together. I also did my best to impart my local knowledge of where to buy equipment and of course, where to get something good to eat. This was particularly easy in Dubai as yet again we were within walking distance of the Souk Madinat.

At some point during this trip I began to have doubts about my decision to leave. Hayden and I got on really well and I could see that if I stayed, we would have worked together comfortably. It had even been suggested that I could relocate to Dubai, with Hayden continuing in London. Splitting ourselves over countries and time zones made a lot of sense. It was a tempting offer and easily the closest I've ever come to changing my mind after handing in my notice.

But it wasn't to be. I left Olive as planned, leaving all the IT gear I had wrangled, cared for and in some cases literally sweated over in the capable hands of Hayden. On my final day Simon said such kind words that I was on the verge of tears. My friend Tim spotted this and casually put me in a head lock to shake me out of it. Thanks Tim.

PART FOUR

AFRICA

CHAPTER TWENTY-FIVE

The weirdest interview

The company attracting me away from Olive was called Drum Cussac. They had broadly the same outlook and make up of staff as Olive but with a more maritime flavour. They had also, at that point at least, completely avoided being sucked into the Middle East and instead operated in other places, including Africa.

I ended up having two interviews with them, the first of which was perfectly ordinary. I met the company founder, Jeremy, while sitting outside a cafe in Hereford. It was gloriously sunny and the meeting was relaxed. Jeremy was charming and just a little bit posh as he explained their dilemma.

Drum Cussac had an ongoing project with Exxon Mobil, based in Nigeria. They had a number of staff out there fulfilling a variety of roles and largely the project was stable. One role had, apparently, consistently failed to be filled though and they'd had a steady flow of people arrive and then leave pretty promptly. It was a technical role and so far, anyone technical enough to be able to do the role hadn't been able to put up with Nigeria. They'd tried others who'd been able to stomach the environment but not been able to do the job.

I was, apparently, just what they were looking for. I was technically competent and came equipped with the ability to 'rough it' in a challenging environment. On paper at least, I appeared to be just what they needed. Was I interested?

It had some appeal to me at the time, particularly considering what I was struggling with at Olive due to the increasingly intense workload. Mostly it was about timing. With the role Jeremy was offering, I would have to work hard, but I'd also be able to have proper time off. It was actually a back-to-back role, with two people alternating between working and enjoying a holiday in between. Officially it was four weeks of each, but when you factored in the travel time and a short handover, it was more like five weeks of work and three weeks of break.

After all the graft I'd had with Olive, the idea of a regular three weeks off was very attractive! While in Nigeria I'd have to work seven days a week, but I'd also be paid for seven days a week, so I should be able to fill my bank account up a little bit. Jeremy told me that everything would be paid for, such as accommodation and food, so apart from a little beer money, it would cost me almost nothing while I was out there. There were a great many unknowns, but I was clearly feeling adventurous as this was part of the appeal.

I had some reservations about working for an 'evil' oil company. I justified it to myself on the grounds that as I happily put petrol in my car, I was already supporting oil companies. Would working for one be all that different? I also felt it was worth seeing what an oil company got up to myself before judging them too harshly. While I'm not unhappy with my judgement at the time, I would choose differently now.

Given the stream of people before me, Jeremy was keen to get some sort of commitment. I agreed that if I came on board, I'd stay for a minimum of one year. To motivate me towards this, Jeremy proposed that I would accrue a small bonus for each day I worked that only paid out once I'd completed a year.

While Jeremy headed up the business, he had little to do with the actual project in Nigeria. For my second interview, I was asked to meet with George who actually worked out there. This was to be the complicated bit!

George also worked on a back-to-back basis, and when not in Nigeria, home for him was Atlanta, Georgia. He would typically shuttle through Heathrow on his way backwards and forwards, so we arranged for me to meet him in between his flights on his way home.

And so, a few weeks later, I found myself on the first tube train of the day on the Jubilee line heading out to Heathrow. While I wasn't so keen on the early start it did mean that I would be able to make it back to London and the Olive office before nine.

George and I met in a coffee shop at the Arrivals area of Heathrow airport, with both of us looking as weary as the other travellers at that early hour. It was an odd place and time to be interviewed, but George was friendly and answered the many questions that I had. In the safety of the airport, over a hot chocolate and a sticky bun masquerading as breakfast, Nigeria seemed mysterious and exotic. I doubt I'd use those two words to describe Nigeria now, but that was how it felt at the time. I said 'Yes'.

CHAPTER TWENTY-SIX

Practicing for a kick in the balls

I enjoyed about three weeks off between leaving Olive and starting with Drum Cussac. This gave me time to relax a bit, get a few things ready and wait for my visa to return from the Nigerian Embassy.

My new route to work was a little bit convoluted. I would fly from Heathrow to Lagos, arriving in the evening. From there I'd stay in Lagos overnight before catching an Exxon owned flight to Eket, my final destination. Nigeria is roughly box shaped, with Lagos in the bottom left-hand corner and Eket in the bottom right, so the second flight covered almost the width of the country.

First then, get to Lagos. Such is the flow of travellers to and from Lagos, that British Airways, Virgin, Air France and Lufthansa each flew a daily flight from Europe. They all arrived within an hour or two of each other, early in the evening. Everyone from Drum used British Airways and our contract with Exxon allowed us the luxury of business class seats.

Luckily for my first trip I had a guide in the form of Ken. He was also going to be my 'back-to-back', the person I would share my job with. Ken was ex-military and had been working on the Exxon project for a few years already. He met me at Heathrow and kindly showed me how to find essential things like the business class lounge. Ken also showed me routines that the team enjoyed, like grabbing a selection of newspapers and magazines to take along for sharing.

This was my first experience with business class and the lounge at least wasn't disappointing. It's hard to go wrong with free food and booze, although free might not be entirely accurate given the increased price of the ticket. The plane was also pretty good, although I think BA reserve their most worn-out planes for the route in and out of Lagos. That didn't matter to me at all and I enjoyed the novelty of the attentive service and food served on plates instead of plastic trays.

I always get nervous in the queue for passport control and arriving in Lagos for the first time was no exception. Drum had a certain number of slots for visas and they were a pain to change the details for. Thus, the job title on my visa had nothing to do with my actual work and I was worried about being questioned.

I was also a bit nervous because some of the information I had written on my arrival slip was false. I'd been warned not to use my real address under any circumstances. The suggestion was to invent an almost real one that would be easy to remember and repeat, so that the information I gave on repeated forms was at least consistent, if inaccurate. Thus, I'd invented and memorised a non-existent address similar to my old address in London. At least I hope it wasn't real otherwise someone might have received some really odd post.

I shouldn't have been concerned, my passport, slip and visa were given a scant glance before receiving the necessary stamp and I was officially in the country.

The next job was to collect my baggage, which wasn't as straightforward as it should have been. It was the same principle as most airports, you stand impatiently waiting while bags pirouette around the carousel for yours to turn up. It was just that in Lagos, the chances of your bag disappearing between the aeroplane and reaching your hands were greatly increased. Or sometimes just some of the contents.

I used a sort of traveller's rucksack at the time, with shoulder straps which could be zipped away and hidden. All the zips had little eyelets so you could use those miniature padlocks if you felt they'd do any good. I was worried that they'd just attract attention, so I opted for something a little more subtle. I'd used zip ties to close up all the compartments in the hope that they would still be tricky for someone in a hurry. As I couldn't carry anything sharp with me onboard, this would also stop me from getting in, so I'd tucked away a folding multi-tool in a small side pocket of the bag. I'd prevented a casual break-in, but for a determined attacker, I'd actually provided them with a means to get in. I waited at the carousel hoping that my plan had worked. It had and I was successfully reunited with all my belongings. The next member of the Drum team travelling through a few days after us wasn't so lucky and he'd had all his underwear stolen, which he wasn't too pleased about.

The next stage was where things got a bit crazier. There were two possible choices for the next stage. Plan A was the official Exxon route, which was to be collected by minibus and taken to a guesthouse for the night. Plan B was the alternative and very unofficial Drum option, which was to be collected by a local driver and taken to the Intercontinental Hotel. As I would learn later, Plan B was definitely the preferred option. However, there was always the potential for this to go wrong, so for my first trip I was to take the official route. This meant I would know what to do in case anything went wrong with Plan B. Ken would be taking the

Drum option and leave me at the airport.

George described trying the official Exxon version as "like practising for a kick in the balls". He wasn't wrong, it wasn't the greatest way of experiencing a new country.

Murtala Muhammed International Airport, to use the official name for the main airport in Lagos, is a fairly hectic place. There were enormous numbers of people milling around in the departures area, but that's nothing compared to how many were waiting outside. It was around eight or nine in the evening by then. It was still hot and humid and there was a mass of people, seemingly with the chief aim of haranguing new arrivals as they tried to make their way out.

Some were beggars, some tried to sell their wares and others were offering to trade currency. The Exxon team were waiting, identifiable by grubby but obvious one-piece, coloured overalls. Other oil companies had similarly dressed individuals but in different colours. Ken waved goodbye as the Exxon team helped me to push through the throng and find a seat in a waiting minibus. We then had to wait to make sure we'd collected everyone from all the flights, not just the one I'd arrived on. While we waited, we were played a tape about the dangers of malaria, which constituted the one and only bit of official health and safety advice I received during my entire trip.

To make sure we didn't miss anyone, we waited for quite a while, lengthened by the heat. While I was used to desert conditions, the humidity was new and it always takes a little bit of time to re-acclimatise anyway. Eventually we set off with an escort of armed and loud Nigerian Police. They travelled in vehicles in front of us and behind, with large horns making whooping noises to get people out of our way.

I don't remember much from that first road trip through Lagos, other than the drama of our escort. With horns blaring almost constantly and blue lights flashing, it seemed to overwhelm the other sites and sounds.

We stopped at a number of locations to drop people off, with me being one of the last stops. My destination was to be an Exxon-owned guesthouse, essentially a free hotel for Exxon employees and contractors with the appropriate privileges. We fitted into this category and were known as 'hatted-contractors'. This meant that we had almost all the same access to Exxon facilities as a regular employee. Other contractors without the same position had to make their own arrangements for transport, accommodation, security and so on. Having a figurative Exxon hat was definitely worth having, at least compared with the alternative.

Not that you would consider my room for the night much of a privilege. It was pretty rough in the bedroom, but the real shock was the bathroom. It looked positively ruined. While water did flow from the taps and the toilet worked, it didn't have much else going for it. More tiles had fallen off the wall into the shower tray than remained on the wall. It was unusable. I ditched the idea of getting a wash and instead headed down to find something to eat.

I don't know what I was expecting to find, but the small buffet I was presented with looked quite good. I didn't even worry too much when I was told it was goat curry. The taste however wasn't so appealing. As I was quite hungry, I tried everything on offer, but I struggled to eat much of anything. It just didn't seem to sit well with my palate. I'm generally not that fussy an eater, but I just couldn't manage to tolerate this. Leaving the safety of the compound to find a chippy wasn't an option either.

I returned to my room, more than a little unhappy with a still half-empty stomach. Despite the cost, I placed an international call to my girlfriend from my mobile. I confirmed that I'd arrived safely and then told her my woes. I don't think I cried that evening, but I was pretty close to it.

I was beginning to think I'd made an enormous mistake. This probably makes me sound like a pretty wimpy traveller, but despite the rough edges with Olive, I'd always been well fed and had a reasonable place to retreat to when necessary. I know some people live in far worse conditions than those I'd been presented with that evening, but at the time, I was feeling pretty sorry for myself.

Ken's journey that evening was quite different, I would get to experience it on my next trip. In complete contrast to the very overt display of force by the police surrounding the minibus, Ken was very much taking the covert route. He was collected by a local man in his car for the drive across Lagos. The advice was to wear a cap pulled down low and sit in the middle of the back seat, so as to be less visible. Lagos has numerous toll gates and these act as pinch points for the traffic. At each one, swarms of people mill around trying to sell things or the seemingly universal offer to wipe your windscreen.

A white face is a particularly interesting target. The greater threat than selling you junk you don't want is that you or your luggage are hauled out towards some unknown fate. Hence the suggestion to try and stay out of sight as much as possible.

The Intercontinental is fairly below par by international standards but palatial by local ones. The normal sized room was usually decorated with an oversized basket of fruit and a bottle of red wine. Standard routine was to take the red wine out in the morning and give it to the driver as a tip. Personally, I preferred to stay in my room and get something to eat. Ken would hit the bar and try to make friends with the flight crews that also usually stayed there. He also got to enjoy a fully functioning bathroom.

Meanwhile I was back in my dingy room. It was pretty late by the time I finally got to bed, but I was still up early in the morning to catch my next flight. The same arrangement with the minibus and police escort took me and a bunch of others to a small corner of another airport for our next flight. Ken was there waiting for me, despite sporting a hangover. This aircraft was pretty small, with single seats only on either side of the aisle and carrying perhaps up to twenty passengers. Nothing bigger than a single paperback book was allowed on the flight and everything else had to go in the hold, including all electronic devices.

I looked on nervously as my precious and delicate electronics were loaded onto a trolley and were carted to the plane. After a great deal of consideration while still at home, I'd decided to take the risk and had brought along my laptop and a DSLR camera on my trip. The laptop came with me again, but the camera remained at home after the first trip.

I can never picture that aeroplane without recalling a cut scene in Indiana Jones where the progress of a plane (and our hero) is denoted by an animated red line carving across a map to the sound of noisy propellers and theme music. While our plane might have been more modern, it didn't feel any more reliable for it than the 1930s aircraft shown in the movies. It also helped that the door to the cockpit was left open for most of the flight, so we had a good view of the instrument deck and any red lights which may or may not have been flashing at the time.

The flight took around eighty minutes and hugged the coastline as we flew over villages and jungle. The landing was pretty easy and our destination airstrip was pretty small. I think the daily flight to and from Lagos was the sum total of the flight traffic most days.

For no particular reason, our passports were inspected once again and our bags were handed over. No chance of our luggage getting 'lost' this time as they were in full view the whole time from the aircraft to the small terminal building less that twenty metres away.

I was introduced to our driver, Anietie who drove us to our hotel to drop off our bags. Anietie, I would soon learn, was a gift and a real help in making life in Nigeria somewhat more tolerable. Almost all foreign workers in Nigeria are provided with a driver and while it sounds rather pompous, it makes a lot of sense.

Driving in Nigeria is quite a different experience to driving back in the UK. While there are plenty of junctions, there are no roundabouts or traffic lights, at least in the part of Nigeria in which I'd just arrived. Road priority is determined less by your positioning and the junction and more by assertiveness and how much you can honk your horn. And Nigerian drivers honk their horn a lot.

The biggest advantage to having a driver was one of liability. If an accident were to happen, we were sagely informed that, as a seemingly rich foreign worker, we would always be held liable regardless of where the fault lay. It wasn't worth the risk of getting in trouble with the authorities and potentially dealing with a large fine because someone else had seen fit to drive into you.

It also provided someone local with a job, something that was deemed beneficial, partly due to the unusual organisational structure in play. In the Middle East and elsewhere, the government owns the oil. They then contract the actual retrieval of the oil to a large multinational like ExxonMobil or Shell. Some foreign labour is brought in to organise things and other foreign labour to do the dirty work. Typically, the locals have relatively little to do with the operation, other than enjoying the large profits. It's a very hands-off approach and seems to work very efficiently.

This was completely at odds with the organisational structure in effect in Nigeria. The Nigerian government insisted on a more involved approach. In our case, the operation was run by a company called Mobil Producing Nigeria (MPN), which was 60% owned by the Nigerian Government and 40% by Exxon Mobil. This meant that, for better or worse, locals worked at all levels of the company. Certain jobs would be entirely filled by locals which in other countries would have been done by imported labour. And of course, this led to a certain amount of job creation in order to satisfy and pacify the population local to the oil.

Maintaining a fleet of drivers employed large numbers of locals and also provided a useful service to foreign workers like myself that couldn't be trusted to drive themselves around, due to our own incompetence or because we might become a target.

On arrival at the hotel, Ken introduced me to a number of figures. I met the hotel manager and reception staff (all bored) as well as a porter who doubled as the laundry service. I gave over my fictitious address again and officially registered my temporary residence in the hotel.

On the way to the room, the porter said he liked my bag and asked me to buy him one when I was back in the UK. He'd happily pay me whatever the price was. Ken casually shook his head from behind the man's shoulder, suggesting that in no way was I to commit to such a task. This, I would learn, was a common request and I was routinely asked to bring things in, such as my footwear, any other visible clothing and even my laptop. I don't think I was ever asked to bring in something that wasn't in sight at the time.

The room was quite large, with a double bed, desk, chair and even a pair of small sofas. I have no idea why anyone thought I might need five separate places to sit down. There was also a good sized ensuite and this time all the tiles remained firmly on the wall. Each room also had a TV and VHS recorder as well as sliding doors opening out onto a balcony. The decor was dated but not offensive. Overall, it was very comfortable and much more pleasant than I'd experienced in Lagos. My spirits started to rise again.

CHAPTER TWENTY-SEVEN

Starting the job

Having been exposed to the hotel, it was now time to try the 'office'. The airstrip and hotel were in Eket, a small but sprawling town, inland slightly from the coast. Work was at the nearby Akwa Ibom Terminal, about twenty minutes' drive away and right alongside the sea. The Terminal acted as a staging post for collecting the oil raised out of the ground by a number of offshore oil-rigs. The Terminal was therefore mostly just a lot of large round collection tankers as well as supporting infrastructure for the offshore work and office workers looking after the whole operation.

Many years before there had been a much more thriving community of foreign workers and their families. It was almost exclusively male workers and these full-time Exxon employees had the option of bringing their wives and children along, which a number of them chose to do. Employees lived in the country full-time, rather than fly backwards and forwards like we did. Having a single individual doing a job rather than two on rotation added stability to the work so the company were happy to support the additional cost of having families there. Next door to the hotel was even a small housing estate for the families, with its own pool and community centre, detached houses and a play park. It was protected by fencing and guards, making it look like a cheaper and less effective version of the compound I'd seen in Saudi Arabia. Thanks to the weather, it was a lot greener though, with mown lawns and small pineapple plants forming low hedgerows.

Unfortunately, there had been a deterioration in relations with the locals to the point where the Terminal had been stormed by angry protestors. The hostility had later spilled over to the housing estate. While there had been no fatalities, thankfully, there had still been some minor levels of violence. Workers and their families had been evacuated promptly, never to return.

When the dust had settled and relations improved, a team had visited from head office. Their recommendations had included better access control through a smaller number of guarded gates, limiting who could get in and when. Most people will be familiar with access control these days, as many office staff have to wear an ID badge around their necks during work hours. As well as a visual identifier, the badge can be used as a digital key to open doors, turnstiles and so on.

The contract had been assigned and work had begun in earnest by a large third-party company. Gates were built, turnstiles installed and progress was made. Unfortunately, after a while, further work stalled due to local contractors getting a bit behind. The card readers couldn't be installed onto the wall as it hadn't been built yet.

So, the installers left shouting "let us know when you're ready" as they departed. This was the situation into which I arrived. I was told there were a few minor steps remaining and then the installation would be restarting. Things were likely to kick off again about two weeks after I arrived.

Looking back, I should have read more into the knowing

smiles, but I gamely began enthusiastically learning the ropes. I had to get to grips with the hardware and software that drove the access control system, as well as learn the people and processes that made it all tick. There were small piles of documentation, aiming to support the transition to access control and then run it effectively in future. Ken invited me to read the documents and make modifications where I saw fit.

I read, I learnt and I made myself known to all the right people. I prepared as if it really was all going to happen fairly promptly. It wasn't. Without spoiling the surprise here too much, when I left a year later, it was still 'about two weeks away' from starting.

As I've already explained, Ken and I would normally only work on our own as part of our job split arrangement. Because we'd arrived together, the plan was for him to do a relatively short trip of three weeks or so and for me to stay on. I'd be in country for another four weeks on my own before he came back to take over again. This seemed like a sensible plan and given that I was paid by the day, a lucrative one as well. However, as the weeks went by, I began to realise that things weren't really going to start in the promised fortnight. Or indeed any time soon.

It also became clear that once I'd got to grips with everything related to my immediate task, there wasn't a great deal of stuff to do. Boredom became my chief enemy.

While there were some fairly sizeable office blocks on-site, we'd managed to score our own building, which was both a blessing and a curse. We were in the emergency control centre, a small building with its own facilities which was designed to be a haven and the management epicentre during a significant event. It had a few small rooms, one of which was used by us. In addition to this it had a toilet, a kitchen (in reality just a space with a sink) and the control room, which was just a big room with more telephones and whiteboards around the edge than was normal.

Under most circumstances, it was myself, Ken and an American called Barry. Ken was, by his own admission, a bit of a loner and enjoyed his own company more than that of others. He proudly told me that his favourite posting in the military had been eighteen months in a solitary office on the Falkland Islands, themselves hardly that well populated. Despite his preference for isolation, Ken shared with us his dry sense of humour and was generous with his time while helping me out.

Barry was a totally different character. Sometimes it was hard to shut him up. Barry and I hit it off very well. I enjoyed the company of both of them, which is fortunate given that Ken, Barry and I shared a small office, pretty much all mealtimes and most of our social time together.

The on-site canteen was awful, so I followed the lead of Ken and the others for lunchtime. We would get our food most days from the cafe back in the housing estate in Eket. Despite not having a great deal to do, we had to keep up appearances, so instead of going there ourselves, Anietie would drive back and collect our food for us. Our lunch arrived luke warm each day, but it was still usually better than that served up in the canteen.

I say usually, because sometimes I struggled to eat it. It wasn't even down to weird or just unfamiliar dishes, I would struggle to eat menu items I considered pretty safe, like spaghetti bolognaise or even burger and chips. Initially I didn't know why I found it so unpalatable, until someone explained the likely cause. The locals typically cooked with cheap, raw palm oil. Unlike the palm oil hidden in a lot of the food we consume nowadays, the raw stuff has a fairly pungent and distinctly unpleasant taste. While the cooking team in our restaurants were supposed to use vegetable oil or olive oil, they sometimes went cheap and used palm oil. In fairness, if you're used to it, it probably doesn't make much difference. To me though, it made all the difference. If it had palm oil in it, I would almost always struggle to eat it.

While my tolerance for below-par food improved, I still struggled to the point where I lost quite a lot of weight. This was compounded on later trips when I got food poisoning a couple of times, including one fairly impressive bout of e-coli. I spent around ten days hovering near a toilet eating little and drinking Lucozade to keep my energy levels up.

Even when I was fit and well, there would be several days when the only food I could stomach was breakfast. Once I went for my evening meal so hungry I was convinced I would eat anything they put before me. I was wrong. When the meal arrived, it was so unpalatable that I lost my appetite almost immediately. I went back to my room, miserable, where my hunger returned about half an hour later but without any chance of satisfaction.

I'm confident that those who know me would describe me as pretty unfussy with regards to food, but Nigeria seriously challenged me. It was a medium-sized problem, but one which was added to the pile and really began to get me down. After Ken left, leaving me with even less to do (or at least fewer people to talk to) I was starting to feel pretty low.

I had nothing to keep me occupied and yet I was still contractually obliged to go into work seven days a week. I spoke to Drum colleagues about my lack of work, but they seemed unfazed. I should simply enjoy the absence of workload (and stress as they saw it) and wait it out. I would be needed soon so I just needed to be patient.

For me, it was torturous. The weeks dragged by and I was seriously considering pulling out on the deal I had made with Jeremy to stay for a full year. In the end, I decided to carry on, at least until I had a break back in the UK and could return refreshed to try for a second stint.

CHAPTER TWENTY-EIGHT
419 ways of scamming

It's impossible to discuss life in Nigeria without covering scamming. Sadly, it's become what Nigeria is most famous for. In my experience, it's not unwarranted either, but perhaps not in the way you would think. Or at least, the scams aren't what you might expect. They certainly weren't what I had expected.

The 'typical' Nigerian scam that most people will have heard of (or received) is via email and goes something along the lines of:

"Hello, I'm a rich Nigerian Prince and I'd like to give you a large chunk of my fortune because I think we might be distantly related."

These emails are collectively called 419 scams, a name that originates from Article 419 within the Nigerian Criminal Code. The Article identifies this sort of scam as one where the target is promised a large reward and will be tricked into paying a small amount of money trying to receive the big payout. Obviously, the big payout never arrives.

If you're daft enough to cough up in the first place, it

doesn't end there. You'll be encouraged to pay another small sum and then another. If you think this wouldn't work, the sheer volume of these emails floating around is testament that it does. It's well worth the effort for the scammers and the returns are pretty good.

Oddly, the things that make them an obvious scam to the majority of people are often deliberately placed. The daft plot of the email, spelling mistakes and even the fact that it mentions Nigeria will set off warning flags for most. But for those few that are still drawn in, they've self-selected themselves as being a good potential target. If the scam emails were more difficult to spot, the scammers would have to work harder to weed out those that wouldn't be likely to fall for the eventual scam. The scammers want to make it easy for themselves by only talking to the most gullible and uninformed.

Based on my knowledge of online scamming and my general worldly experience (or what I thought I possessed), I thought I was mentally prepared for possible scams. On first arrival in the country, I treated it much like a tourist might going into a Turkish bazaar; I expected to be approached and sweet-talked into buying an overpriced rug. So long as I kept my wits about me, I wouldn't be out of pocket. As I discovered, I wasn't going to be out of pocket, but I was very wrong about the scammers approach.

The reality of scamming in Nigeria is very different when you're there to the online version. While I was often very much involved in scams (against my will I should add), I was almost never the target. More just a pawn in play really. Ultimately Exxon were the victim in almost all cases (or Mobil Producing Nigeria) but it's my belief that this was understood by the company as a cost of doing business there.

To give you an example, we'll start with my breakfast. While staying at the hotel, I would naturally have breakfast there each day. I would arrive and place my order with a bored looking waitress. I'd usually order scrambled eggs on toast or similar, having learnt in Iraq that you can't eat free sausages and bacon every morning without paying for it later. The waitress would write my order on the pad together with a few extras - *'Scrambled eggs, toast, sausage, bacon, tomatoes'* and take that to the kitchen.

The kitchen would duly make up the order and it would be placed on the counter ready for collection by the waitress. Only at this point, there's twice as much food as I had ordered. The waitress would then, without much subtlety, scrape the extra items off my plate into a waiting doggy bag. The remaining items would be casually rearranged on the plate to try to make the plate look vaguely full again. I would then be served exactly what I'd asked for.

This would happen time and time again to all the diners and yet no one ever complained. I certainly never did. I'm pretty sure some people much more senior would have witnessed this behaviour and I'm also confident that they never confronted anyone about it either. And why not? Because it's only a bit of breakfast and it's always good to try to keep the kitchen and waiting staff on your side. What's a stolen sausage between friends?

But this sort of scam was rife throughout everyday life in Nigeria. I was a witness and sometimes unwillingly or unwittingly along for the ride, but never the victim.

Some of the scams were much larger in scope than this, but still equally successful and unchallenged. For some 64 rooms, I was told the hotel had over 165 members of staff on the books. We had waiting staff, bar staff, a tennis coach, lifeguards and (rumour had it) even one person whose sole responsibility was maintaining the fleet of virtually unused VHS recorders the hotel owned. However almost all of these members of staff were unseen and likely didn't exist. The manager of the hotel was claiming non-existent staff on the books and likely adding their salaries to his own.

Amazingly, we did actually see some lifeguards from time to time. They didn't do much other than sit around and look disappointed with the way their lives had turned out. On the one occasion someone really did get into trouble in the water, and it turned out that the lifeguard couldn't swim. Luckily, they managed to rescue the unfortunate soul by reaching into the pool with a net on a long pole.

The guards would occasionally shout at us for 'dangerous' behaviour, like diving in off the side. One lifeguard even tried to get Dave, one of the Drum security team, out of the pool as he did lengths, which was funny as he was ex-SBS (Special Boat Service) and incredibly well trained at not dying in water. I'm pretty confident he told them to 'Fuck Off' and then ignored further remonstrations.

Inevitably, scamming extended beyond the hotel and to all parts of work and life. As mentioned, the security team were overseeing the access control project, including getting the new ingress and egress buildings finished. As the IT guy, the buildings were well outside my remit, but given that I had little else to do, I would still get involved when I could. Or even just tag along in preference to sitting in the office twiddling my thumbs.

As you may or may not know, it can get pretty wet in that part of the world. Warm and wet air from the seas to the south clash with hot and dry air from the deserts to the north and the result is rain on a biblical level. I've still yet to see persistent rain in the UK of the level you would get in that part of Nigeria on a frequent basis. Storms would often accompany the rain and as the Terminal possessed some of the only tall structures in the area, they attracted a lot of lightening. It was quite a show.

To protect (and keep happy) the people in the expected

queues to get in and out of the Terminal, large sections of sheltered roofing were being constructed. These long, covered walkways were being built while I was there. Only it wasn't going very well.

For work of that nature, just like elsewhere in the world, companies would be invited to tender. Once a company had been selected by the procurement team, they would issue a contract and work would begin. Only the contracts weren't very robust and led to some fairly poor behaviour.

Once, say, 50% of the work had been completed, the company in question would have received at least 70% of the funds they needed to complete the work. At this point, they'd be better off simply pocketing the balance and walking off the job, leaving the work incomplete. So frequently, that's just what they did. This sort of practice was unfortunately common.

I know what you're thinking. Any company that did that would pretty quickly earn a bad reputation and be prevented from further work, thus shooting themselves in the foot. That wasn't the case in Nigeria.

A company in the UK, for instance, is registered with Companies House, along with a record of the directors. The directors in turn are also identifiable, possessing a birth certificate, passport and so on. If a company, its staff or whoever are particularly naughty, a victim can rely on the police or the court system to even things out for them. No, it's not perfect, but in the majority of cases it's sufficient to either sort things out or simply to prevent bad behaviour in the first place.

If you strip away all the checks and balances that make up this grand system, you've got yourself a bit of a problem. A company that misbehaves can simply become a new company. The directors can have new names. There is little in the way of tracking and if you don't have a system like this in place, it's not the sort of thing you can simply kick-off when you need to. It needs to be built up over years and largely already running in order to make use of it.

So in the case of our walkway, a new contract would have to be raised to get the job finished. And there was nothing stopping the original company that had walked off the job to tender to come back in and finish the job off. They could therefore be paid again to do the job that they'd already been paid (at least in part) to do in the first place. Knowing they could be paid a second time was another incentive to walk off the first job.

Rather than having a system which dissuaded people from doing this sort of thing, the system in Nigeria positively encouraged it. So the same company would come back in, and yet again, walk off the job before it was finished. And so on, meaning that pretty much any project took far longer and cost far more than it should do. No wonder there weren't any walls to screw the access card readers to.

All the scamming had a very real effect on Nigerian wealth through oil. Exxon greased the right wheels just enough to get the oil flowing out of the ground and onto container ships. But crude oil isn't worth nearly as much as refined oil, so it needs to be sent to a refinery first. This is where Exxon gave up on Nigeria and simply shipped the oil to refineries elsewhere.

The story I heard was that Nigeria had twelve of its own refineries, but that none of them were operational. It wasn't in Exxon's interest to get them running as it was cheaper to have the oil refined somewhere they had more control and didn't have to pay extra to counter the effect of institutional scamming. They left the running of the refineries entirely to the Nigerians, which meant they remained out of action. I can imagine the official line was something like,

"Of course! We'd love to refine the oil here. Just let us know as soon as that refinery is up and running and we'll bring the oil over. But for now......"

Exxon made more money (or lost less) from having the oil processed elsewhere and Nigeria lost out as a result. Nigeria gave up control of the oil while it was still crude and therefore made a lot less money. In most countries, petrol is taxed heavily at the pump, partly because of environmental reasons, but also because it's probably an easy taxation point. Because the average Nigerian expects to benefit from the country's oil wealth, petrol was actually subsidised at the pump, making it cheaper to buy than it was to produce. And this was despite the refining taking place elsewhere, greatly reducing the profit the Nigerian government made on oil production.

It's hard to blame Nigerians personally for the lack of western institutional systems (birth certificates, company registers, etc) which would help to reduce scamming. We try to rely on something that isn't there. In any society, a small number of individuals will always try to take advantage and stretch a few rules. It's just that in Nigeria it happens to be a lot easier to do so and there are fewer repercussions. While we might complain in the UK about bureaucracy, we don't tend to think about the benefits of the systems that we rely on and the trust we place in contracts, companies and people by extension.

So long as Nigeria continues to lack the systems and bureaucracy that we enjoy, scamming at a local and national level will continue. And so long as people are willing to believe that an unknown Nigerian relative wants to send them a fortune, so will the emails.

CHAPTER TWENTY-NINE

The corpse's trousers

Despite the lack of things to do, I had been trying to do my best. When Ken returned at the end of my second trip, we went through the changes I'd made to the documentation. Despite suggesting that I reviewed them and make changes, it would seem that Ken wasn't really all that receptive to change after all, and reverted almost of all my amendments.

I can't really blame Ken for this, he'd been there for years at this point and didn't really feel the need for anyone to rock the boat. But it was hardly motivating for me to do further work when I knew almost all of it would all be rejected.

Regardless of Ken's views on change, there were minor improvements to be made, so I plodded on anyway. One interesting problem was related to the electricity supply, or lack of it. In most situations where cards are relied upon to allow entry to buildings, they are wholly relied upon as a single source of truth. But that only works while everything has power from the readers on the wall to the computers that control everything in the background. In our part of Nigeria, power cuts were very common and they didn't have any sort of backup generator to rely on. So any ID card had to work with or without the electronic readers in action.

They already had ID cards, but these were just plain plastic and didn't work electronically. They were very colourful though, with a plethora of colours used to identify different departments and so on. This is counter to most ID badges that are deliberately plain and contained the minimum of information required to confirm the owner of the badge. There were so many colours on the company badges that the guards couldn't possibly remember what they all stood for and explanatory posters were placed on the walls in guardhouses as a helper.

Which department an individual belonged to would help the guards to know (assuming they cared) when access was allowed. An office worker would typically only need access during office hours, whereas an engineer might need access at any time to go and fix something. The security team tried to limit access when it wasn't required because that often led to theft, particularly on the weekends when it was normally quieter.

When each department was asked to categorise access by time, the resulting mess was a huge list of all possible options ranging from 'all the time' to 'most Wednesdays and every second Tuesday in the month'. It was impossible for the guards to know all this and no way to display it succinctly on a badge.

In order to simplify matters, I reduced the options to four, derived from two options each between Monday to Friday or all week and office hours or 24 hours. The result could be displayed as a single box highlighted in a 2x2 square. The argument being that although it was a slightly blunt instrument in terms of limiting the options, it also made it much simpler to implement. The box could be displayed on all badges, it worked when there wasn't power and it was simple enough to be universally understood.

Bizarre as this might sound, this simple box was probably

my crowning achievement during my time in Nigeria. The push back I received about it from various directions gave me purpose, something to argue about and a job to do. I was, in hindsight, overly committed to demonstrating that my suggestion was the correct course of action, when in reality the majority of people didn't give a toss. I wrote procedural documents on how to determine legitimate access from the now depleted options. I created forms for applicants to complete and to get authorised. I kept myself occupied rather than go mad with nothing to do.

I'm still proud of my box idea. Although the end result was incredibly simple, that was the point. And yet, it comes with a shade of embarrassment, that this should be the highlight of a year's work in a foreign country. I have no idea whether or not my suggestion was ever implemented.

With regards to the existing badges, Ken and I started to stick our noses more into the existing setup. There was a badging office which was deliberately slightly remote from the main gate. This kept the additional queues and cars away from causing a blockage. We would go round there routinely to help them out or possibly just stick our noses in.

The badging office was staffed by three or four people whose job it was to issue badges out only to those with a legitimate need accompanied by the proper paperwork. This being Nigeria, having a suitable bribe was also a very possible path to obtaining a badge. Although we didn't know for sure, we were reasonably confident only one of the staff in the badging office was accepting the bribes, but we had no proof. In fairness, we had no remit to do anything about it either, but I'm sure we could have made a fuss. At the very least, we hoped our presence, help and oversight would limit their options for handing out dodgy badges.

It wasn't just one or two extra people wandering around site either. MPN had a canteen for local workers and free lunch was available every day. Around lunchtime, the site was busier to the tune of an estimated one thousand extra people, a staggering number. All of these people had either legitimately obtained a badge and then failed to return it or should never have had one in the first place.

I've no idea how many extra kitchen staff were needed to feed all these extra mouths, but it must have been quite significant. Regardless of the security benefits, the enhanced access control system could more than pay for itself simply in the reduction of the daily food bill.

With a view to smoothing the path of transition to the new badging system, I had also been working on transferring data from the old terminal in the badging office. The data was a mess, and I spent countless hours doing data entry and attempting to understand the muddle. Yet again, we had the struggle of trying to fit local Nigerian information (or lack of it) into a system designed for a different culture. According to the data I had to work with, many individuals lacked a date of birth or even a surname. The new badging system required both so there were an enormous number of people that shared the same birthday of 1st January.

In the event that an individual lacked a surname (at least according to the data I had), then normally someone had simply repeated their first name in the field. It was also fairly common practice for individuals to be named after the day they were born, so we had plenty of people listed with the name Monday, Tuesday etc. If they also lacked a surname, they would be entered in as 'Monday Monday'. This never failed to trigger the well-known song by The Mamas and Papas in my head. I'm pretty sure you've got it in your head now and if you haven't, get onto YouTube quick, it's a real ear worm!

For a break from data entry, I would jump at the chance to go around the site. Barry's role was to look at the physical security and ensure gates, fences, cameras and even lights were being put up in the right place and facing the right direction. He would help to plan new parts and monitor existing builds to ensure they were being done to the plan (assuming they were being done at all). Barry would kindly invite me along most times that he needed to do some sort of inspection. Or sometimes just when he fancied some company while going for a walk.

Getting around the site could be an amusing challenge in itself. To start with, all the services needed to run the site (electricity, water, cabling, etc) had been buried in the ground. But either no record had been kept as to their location or the records had been lost, and therefore no one knew where they were. Over time, as the site grew and changed, new service lines needed to be installed. After a few accidents where lines were cut or damaged, it was decided that digging into the ground was too risky without knowing where existing services ran.

This meant that any new lines ran above ground, regardless of the inconvenience. It was quite common to find a large pipe running alongside a path take a ninety degree turn right across it. You would have to take big steps over the pipes, carrying on your stride as if this was perfectly normal. Which in Nigeria, it was.

This led to some unexpected behaviours and more job creation. Because pipes, conduits and even taps could be poking out almost anywhere, it wasn't possible to cut the grass with a lawn mower. It would be dangerous to the operator and a problem for the site in general. Instead, the grass was cut by hand by teams of men armed with machetes. It must have been back-breaking work and, just like painting the Forth bridge, it needed to be done continuously and in all weathers. It also meant that seeing people walking around site brandishing machetes was perfectly normal.

Despite the trip hazards, I would accompany Barry on important tasks like 'counting the chairs in the such-and-such building' or 'seeing if the hole cut in the fence over there has gotten any bigger'. Sometimes Barry would be doing slightly more technical work and I would hang around and try to learn. I didn't pick up nearly enough to be proficient, but I certainly understood a lot more about things like the placement of fences and how that might affect flows of people.

And when I wasn't wandering around outside, I would get a small but steady stream of visitors. I would like to claim that they were dropping by for my scintillating conversation, but often they were just dropping by to drop something off.

Our office was unusual in that it was locked to outsiders, in order to preserve the sanctity of the emergency control room. Thus, compared to the rest of the site, our toilet was greatly underused and a much better state as a result. We even had our cleaner whose full-time job was to look after four rooms (one of which was always locked), a short corridor and the toilet. Most of the time she just went to sleep in the tiny kitchen.

Several times a day I would have to let visitors in so that they could come in for a dump. It wasn't exactly a members' club, they just had to know me well enough to not be embarrassed about the reason for their visit. Most times they would hang around for a chat too, helping to break up my day. Barry had been moved to a different office after a couple of months, so most of the time I was otherwise completely on my own so I welcomed the interruption.

After I had been in the country on and off for about six months, I got two unexpected visitors that hadn't just come to use the bog. They were two Americans from Exxon's head office in Houston and they were performing a health and safety check – would I object to being interviewed? I didn't need to check my calendar to know I was available so I happily agreed to chat with them.

They were particularly interested to know what health and safety guidance I'd received since arriving and how useful I'd found it. It wasn't a long list for me to recall, it started and ended with the tape about malaria precautions I'd heard on the minibus the night I'd arrived. I had received no formal training or guidance since then. Although clearly the security team were helping me out and making sure I didn't do anything too stupid.

The Americans were horrified and reeled off a huge list of training I should have been subjected to, from kidnap awareness to the right way to sit at my desk. They left promising that the situation would be rectified and I groaned inwardly at the likely hours I would have to spend looking at PowerPoint presentations. I never heard from them again and I wasn't invited to a single minute of extra training either.

Perhaps this wasn't entirely true – I had attended one other training course. The Spy Police (more on them later) had monthly training sessions, and as I was a member of the security team, I was also obliged to attend. The first one I went to was a real eye opener. As an apparently senior member of the team, I was placed on a table at the front of the meeting facing the crowd. I wasn't expecting this and it meant I couldn't quietly nod off while all eyes were upon me.

The hour-long meeting contained various routine notices before an 'expert' then stood up to talk about daily hazards and what to do about them. He mentioned things like dripping air-con units (slip hazard) and fast-moving vehicles (obviously the pedestrians' fault if they didn't get out of the way) but the highlight of the talk was his discussion of the famous Heimlich Manoeuvre.

This, as you will likely know from various sources, is to help someone that is choking by forcibly dislodging the blockage. The trainer kicked off by describing the scenario 'A man eats too many potatoes and can't breathe. What would you do?' and welcomed suggestions from the audience.

A great discussion started with the consensus being that the careless consumer of potatoes should be loudly and strongly berated for eating too fast. This may have fallen on deaf ears, particularly for the potato fan who would presumably have expired in front of them, regretting too late the reason for his plight. As serious as it was, I struggled not to grin through the various ridiculous ideas. It became sillier still though, as the trainer proceeded to talk about how you should really go about helping our hapless and theoretical victim.

I've never since seen someone spend so much time talking about something while managing to convey so little detail or information about the subject in hand. At no point did the trainer demonstrate how to perform the manoeuvre or accurately describe how it should be done. If I hadn't already known about it, I too wouldn't have had the first clue what he was talking about, and even with some knowledge it was difficult to follow. Suffice to say, I never attended another of the monthly briefs.

It is yet another assumption we (or at least I) have about life in other countries. It's kind of accepted that everyone has a certain amount of first aid knowledge, even if they don't know how it should be applied. But that just isn't always the case.

Courtesy of medical shows on TV, we all know that there is a recovery position, even if we don't know how to do it. We would understand enough to go and find help from someone that does know rather than simply having a go. And in the event of a serious accident, we know not to move the injured party until a trained medic arrives (unless by leaving them they remain in harm's way). This seems common sense, and yet in reality it's information we've had the privilege of learning, even if we can't identify how and when.

I witnessed the aftermath of a road traffic accident where a motorcyclist had been knocked off. Instead of treating the injured party cautiously and gently, he was hauled to his feet, head lolling. In order to help the poor man, others then started to pump his arms up and down vigorously, appearing as though they were helping him to take flight. There were perhaps half a dozen people involved in this horror of a rescue. Perhaps they intended to hasten his rise to the Almighty. Due to fear for our own safety, we didn't stop or interfere. Although we might think we know better, it's not always welcomed.

I saw a number of small accidents on the roads but the worst was seeing a corpse at the side of the road near the airstrip. I'd only just arrived so it was a shocking welcome back. According to my colleagues who had kindly met me that day, the victim had already been there for a few days. He was still there a couple of days later when it was my turn to act as welcoming party. But this time someone had stolen his shoes and trousers. Apart from the indignity of being left for dead on the roadside, the poor man was now naked from the waist down.

I could only hope that if I met an untimely demise while there, someone would at least let me keep my trousers on.

CHAPTER THIRTY

Not becoming a racist

One thing I didn't expect to try in Nigeria was car maintenance. With all the foreign workers with their drivers as well as general purpose vehicles, MPN owned a sizeable fleet. A lot of the vehicles were regular saloon cars, typically Toyotas. For some reason almost all the backup vehicles were pickups, usually small and uncomfortable. MPN outsourced the vehicle maintenance to a local firm and yet again, a small flaw in the contract became an opportunity to be exploited.

Firstly, the contract insisted that all spare parts were genuine. In a country awash with fakes, this could delay any repairs for weeks as the parts had to be sourced and delivered, probably from overseas. To allow for inevitable delays, a daily charge was levied for storing the vehicles in a secured area. This incentivised the maintenance company to do, well nothing. The longer they had a vehicle in their compound, the more money they could charge for not doing anything to it.

We were used to any minor repair or service taking at least two weeks. It was just one of the inconveniences you got used to. After a brake service, our car came back making some horrendous noises every time Anietie pressed the brake pedal. He was going to take it straight back, but we weren't keen to spend another fortnight in one of the bouncy pickups.

With Anietie watching us with a look of real concern, Barry and I jacked the car up and took the wheel off. The brake calliper should have been held in place with two fairly substantial bolts. Instead, it was rather ineffectively held on with just one, and each time the brake was used, it was pivoting until it bumped into something, hence the loud noise.

We removed the remaining bolt so that Anietie could use it to find a match somewhere in town, in a borrowed car obviously. He was gone less than an hour before he returned bearing a spare bolt. We fitted it all back together and the car was safely up and running again. Anietie's original look of consternation had flipped to one of absolute delight. Apparently, he was genuinely impressed that we could (or would) turn our hands to a bit of car maintenance. I don't think he liked the pickups either.

Writing now, it can seem petty to complain about having to use a different car or that my meals weren't always great. In isolation, any of these events would be trivial, but when you're dealing with this sort of thing several times a day, it can become very draining. In Iraq and elsewhere in the Middle East, you could have a difficult day, but still retire to something at least reasonably homely at the end of it. By comparison, Nigeria often offered little respite; even in the hotel room we would face power cuts or a lack of hot water. There was no escape.

It was hard not to take it all a little personally. It's not just that things would break or go wrong, there were people behind these things whose job it was to keep them functioning. Only they often didn't do their jobs very well. Our collective difficulties were frequently attributable to someone being incompetent, lazy or simply avoiding doing a proper job as part of some scam or other.

It was about the time I'd put all this together, somewhere in my first or second trip, that I began to really worry that I had become a racist. I'd witnessed some fairly stark racism in the Middle East with some of the less pleasant Olive team members referring to locals as 'Monkeys' or worse. At the time it had shocked and disgusted me, and I was now worried that I had become a part of that same dark corner.

Like the old adage that you're not really paranoid if everyone really is out to get you, it was hard not to feel under attack when daily life is unnecessarily difficult due in large part to the typical attitudes and behaviours of the local population. When you recognise that these behaviours are sadly true for a lot of people, the dangerous next step is how you treat anyone you then meet based on this. You go from recognising that someone might be a scammer to assuming they are. A sensible security stance is to assume the worst, but it's not always the best position with regards to getting along with people or simply not tarring everyone with the same brush.

Ultimately, I decided that I wasn't a racist because I didn't want to be. Everyone has unconscious biases that they act on, none of us can help that. The difference is the effort you put into recognising these biases in yourself, challenging them and then trying to change your own approach. So long as I did my best to continue to challenge my own assumptions, I would not be or consider myself to be a racist.

Part of this decision was also to recognise the Nigerians I had met that were good people and therefore that the assumption couldn't always be true. At the top of this list was Anietie. He was an absolute star and genuinely did his best to look after us. I really felt like he was part of the team and had our best interests at heart.

One great example of Anietie's protectiveness towards us

was his attitude towards roadworks. The regular downpours weren't kind to the roads, which were largely tarmac placed directly on top of the sandy soil. Potholes that exposed the sand underneath could get deep very quickly. As official repairs generally lagged behind the holes by quite a duration, there were always potholes to be navigated on any given journey.

Enterprising youths would fill up the holes with more sand, creating a very short-lived solution. With further road traffic, the sand would soon sink back down, but for a while at least, you didn't drop quite so far into the hole. The problem was that this wasn't really a paid job, so as well as the minor road repairs, they'd also build a far more major speed bump. Any passing car would have to slow down and so the youths would bang on the window and demand money in return for their efforts. It was less community minded and more roadworks with menaces.

Some drivers would slow right down for bumps, giving the demanding youths easy access to us. One driver we sometimes got when Anietie had a day off would even go as far as to wind our windows down from his controls in the front.

"These men will not let us pass until we pay them some money."

And by we, he meant us. In contrast, Anietie would go over the speed bump at the highest safe speed he thought he could get away with, revving and blasting the horn at anyone that got too close to our car.

Anietie wasn't the only person I met in Nigeria that was kind and genuine but he was definitely the one I had the most to do with. He made the experience a lot better when it could so easily have been made a lot worse. Thanks Anietie.

CHAPTER THIRTY-ONE

In case of emergency, break surf

So far, I've made it sound like my time in Nigeria was *no* work and no play. Total boredom other than dealing with annoyances and, to start with, it was like that. Slowly, I began to realise that there were social aspects to living in Nigeria that I wasn't taking part in. It was simply a case of asking around, talking to the right people and inviting yourself along.

One of the first small social scenes I discovered was the small group that routinely tested the water-based emergency evacuation vehicles. I've no idea how they managed to get these purchased by the company and all the way out to Nigeria, but the vehicles consisted of a speedboat and two jet skis. They were clearly toys and almost certainly completely useless in a real evacuation. Not that I was complaining, they were fantastic fun. While Eket was only near the coast, not on it, we were right next to one of the enormous tributaries that form the Niger Delta.

It's hard to explain the size of the river, you just have to see it to fully experience it. Suffice to say, it was incredibly wide and remains by far the biggest river I've seen with my own eyes. On top of that, there were smaller branches of various sizes feeding the main section up and down from where we were.

Riding a jet ski is a little confusing at first, mainly because there's no brake. You can either slow down by lifting off the throttle, or preferably, simply turn it and shoot off in a different direction. This sounds simple, but if you're heading a bit too rapidly to something solid, pressing the accelerator to help you turn and change direction is not a natural reaction.

Luckily there were plenty of people to give me tips, and I became reasonably proficient. I would never match the skill of the two Australian chaps though. They appeared to have grown up on jet skis and were very talented. The jet skis were large enough to take a pillion and although I enjoyed being in control, sometimes it was more fun to ride on the back with someone that really knew what they were doing. We would shoot off down a small tributary, leaning from side to side and (to my mind at least) looking like an exciting chase scene from a movie.

The speedboat was also a great deal of fun, although I managed to drive that a lot less. We wouldn't normally roam too far in it but sometimes we'd venture further from the launch point. Once you got away from the town a little, it felt incredibly remote with seemingly nothing but jungle either side of the river. I always enjoyed getting out to what felt like wild jungle.

Once we took both jet skis and speed boat all the way downstream and onto the sea. It was a delightful trip to begin with, the sun beating down to the point that I earned myself a bit of sunburn on the top of my unprotected head. The weather turned while we were out and it began to rain heavily. We put one chap who was wearing glasses in charge of the boat as he was the only one that could see without being stung in the eyes as we went along.

Occasionally we would try a different form of transport. There were also three kayaks that we could use. These came out less frequently, but as I'd previously done quite a bit of kayaking, I was always keen to get in one. I have a wonderful photo of myself and another chap called Luke sitting in our kayaks on the river framed by jungle and sunset.

All of this testing of the important evacuation vehicles was thirsty work and the afternoon usually involved a few beers and sometimes a BBQ. You'll be relieved to know that we tested them weekly.

Technically I shouldn't really have attended these weekly afternoon socials as they started at around three while I was still contracted to be at work. No one seemed to care or complain though and I felt a little downtime was reasonably well earned. Plus, the draw of the river was too tempting to ignore.

CHAPTER THIRTY-TWO

Running with hookers

There were a couple of other social events we could attend. One of the local bars, 'Nancy's', served fish and chips on a Friday evening. Unsurprisingly, this was pretty popular with the Brits, including me, although other nationalities were happy to partake. It was a drive across town from the hotel, so in order to get there we would ask Anietie to take us over. As this was definitely not a work necessity, he would transport us in his own car. We tipped him pretty generously for the privilege.

A bit like my experience of Iraq, the satisfaction of a cold beer in a hot country was not to be underestimated. The fish and chips were pretty good too and it could get quite busy. The main issue for me was that it was also very popular with the local prostitutes, known as night fighters. These ladies would come over as soon as you sat down and try to make conversation.

"Good evening, would you like a wife?"

"No thank you, I'm already married" (I actually wasn't at that point, but didn't let facts get in the way of a good excuse)

"Would you like a Nigerian wife?"

"No thank you"

"Don't you like Nigerian women?"

And so on. If they went on too long, conversations like this could really spoil an otherwise relaxing evening.

My preferred tactic was to be polite but otherwise to ignore them as much as possible. I thought I sounded polite yet assertive but I probably sounded like a stuttering Hugh Grant in his romcom heyday. Although I'm pretty sure they wouldn't have known who Hugh Grant was.

Ignoring them seemed sensible; they were after custom after all, and if I wasn't interested, they'd move on to another mark. One of our group, Phil, was under the impression that the best way to get rid of them was to pay them off. Despite our vocal disagreements, he would offer them cash just to go away. If it worked one week, it certainly didn't help them to leave us alone the following week as they would expect another payout.

Nancy's was also the default location for the latter part of the hash runs that took place fortnightly. I hadn't heard of hash runs before and it would seem most people in the UK haven't either, despite the fact that it's incredibly popular with Brits (and others) living abroad. Hash runs originated in Malaysia and the concept was originally created by a group of Brits in 1938, probably while wearing oddly styled colonial hats.

Often known as 'A Drinking Club With A Running Problem', the idea is quite cool really. Someone, known as a hare, goes out in advance and marks a running trail, usually with something that naturally degrades, like flour or shredded paper. The hounds then follow on the route, but rather than simply follow a single trail, the hare can use a range of different marks to denote different things, such as false trails. For example, at a fork in the path, there might be a particular mark 100 metres along denoting that this path is the wrong one. The runners then double back and go down the right path.

The effect of this is to keep the group bunched up. The front-runners take all the wrong routes and rack up more miles. Those further back can catch up and can then follow along the right route without wasting time seeking it out. In the true spirit of the game, it's non-competitive, and runners are encouraged to shout back to those behind them and guide them along the correct route.

The hash attracted a reasonably sized crowd each time. Although it was clearly dominated by foreign workers, locals were welcome too. With a few exceptions, most of the local women that attended were night fighters, making for a more diverse group than your average running club.

The routes varied in location, but it didn't usually matter as it was almost always a load of jungle. I have no idea how the hares set the route, because if it wasn't for the markers and other runners beside me, I would have been completely lost. With only jungle around you and nothing sticking up on the horizon in any direction, it was hard to maintain your bearings.

Still, it was always nice to get out into nature, and just like on the river, it was easy to feel that you were pretty remote from any sort of civilisation. That wasn't always true though, and sometimes the trail would lead through a small village. These would have free ranging goats, chickens and children to get in your way. Typically, the buildings in such villages were noticeably more rudimentary than those we saw in town.

The children would stare as we ran past and often shouted 'White man!' at us as we stumbled and sweated along.

After we'd finished the run, making sure no one was lost

first, we'd head back to our chosen bar, most frequently Nancy's. There we'd embark on the next stage of the hash tradition, the 'Down-down'. This would involve beer and food, but we could only properly relax once the obligatory circle had taken place. We'd stand around, singing a few songs and the Grand Master would pick on a few people to neck their beers. They'd have to accomplish this while everyone else stood around chanting 'down, down, down…'. You don't need to be a genius to figure out where the down-down got its name.

Selection for standing in the middle ranged from getting lost, urinating on (or beside) the trail or generally anything noteworthy that had gotten you noticed. You were entirely at the whim of the Grand Master or anyone else in the crowd willing to stick out their own neck. For this reason, I generally avoided much attention and was perhaps quieter than I would have been otherwise. I was mostly successful and didn't get picked on much, which was a relief as I'm pretty mediocre at drinking beer in a hurry.

My reticence to get noticed most of the time led to my acquiring a rather unusual nickname. On your fifth run, you are officially recognised as a member of the hash and given a hash name. At least that's how it operated at our club. You would be stuck once again in the middle of the circle while various names were shouted out by the crowd as possibilities.

Those that knew me reasonably well seemed not to want to get involved and most of the other workers didn't know me well enough to make a suggestion. Apparently, my plan to hide in plain sight had been a little too successful. The only group that was vocal were the night fighters, who shouted out their suggestion very loudly.

"Slow poison" they called repeatedly, "Slow poison!"

The Grand Master looked genuinely at a loss for what to do, but in the absence of any other suggestions, I was duly christened 'Slow poison'. The locals all sniggered at this result while the rest of us stood around looking baffled. None of us had a clue what it meant. For the rest of the evening, I tried to get an explanation but no one seemed keen to let me in on the joke.

The next morning on our way to work, I asked Anietie if he knew what the name meant. I had to explain the context to him, which then drew a large smile. According to the hookers at least, I was only pretending not to be interested in them. They were, apparently, slowly poisoning my mind and in the long run, I would come round to their way of thinking. In short, they were saying that it was only a matter of time before I'd be theirs.

Even if they were wrong about the slow poisoning of my mind, I'm still a little bit proud of my odd nickname. It's pretty funny.

CHAPTER THIRTY-THREE
Chops by chopper

If you're not a foodie, you might not want to bother reading this chapter. My food-related distress might not resonate. Even if you are a foodie, you still might want to skip it. The anguish might be too much for you.

As you can probably tell from my comments in earlier chapters, I was starting to obsess about food. Not having anything you can eat will do that. I was only dealing with the occasional (or frequent) bad meal. I can't imagine what it must be like if you were truly without food for any length of time. It must drive you round the twist. Or to an early grave, obviously.

Particularly on my earlier trips, I would create a fantasy list of things I was going to eat when I got back to the UK. Steak, red wine and pink grapefruit juice invariably topped my list. In reality, eating in Nigeria did become easier over time. There were a few things to learn which could really help. Apart from the restaurant in the hotel, there was also the cafe in the housing estate next door. The restaurant ran their menu on a fortnightly rotation, so you could figure out which meals were okay and which to avoid.

As well as Nancy's, there were other external options too,

including a Chinese restaurant only a short walk away. We didn't go there very often, but it provided a nice break when we were desperate for a change.

I was also able to start building up my own supplies. Because I would always be returning to the same location, there was no reason to heft all my luggage backwards and forwards. I left as much as I could behind, returning to the UK with an almost empty bag. The main benefit was that when I headed out to Nigeria, three quarters of my bag was stocked with food.

You have to be a bit creative when it comes to taking food on an aircraft. You need things that will travel well and keep well whilst also being reasonably light and compact. Pot noodles fit the bill very well and could serve as an easy meal replacement. And if you tape them together top to top, you're much less likely to damage the foil on the top. I'd also take snack items like mini portions of cheese, kept in a small cool bag for the flight. Once or twice, I took something heavier along like a Fray Bentos pie in a tin. If you don't know what these are, you haven't really missed much but under the circumstances they were a delicacy. I'd eke out my treasure trove of food for a month.

There were some things I could buy locally which weren't all that bad. One shop near the Terminal sold chocolate bars and tubes of Pringles. The chocolate was ok, but for some reason always had a mild but noticeable taste of some sort of cleaning fluid. I didn't eat those often. The Pringles tasted fine but despite trying quite a few tubes, I never found a complete crisp. Every single one I ever saw had been smashed somehow, which is quite an achievement.

It was possible to buy booze locally, although we tended just to order at the bar. One exception to this was the single serving sachets of gin and rum which were available. I took a few boxes of these back to the UK, purely for the novelty value of having booze in the sort of sachets normally reserved for ketchup.

Once a week, the hotel restaurant turned on the ice cream machine. It was the sort of machine that would normally be left on all the time, but to save money, they only used it weekly. Apparently, that coupled with a slack cleaning routine had resulted in a few diners getting salmonella poisoning in the past. Given that anything we ate ought to come with a health warning with regards to its preparation, this didn't worry us unduly.

The unwritten rule for ice cream night was "Sit next to an American". Unsurprisingly, the ice cream wasn't actually that good. They skimped on the mixture so it wasn't nearly as creamy or sweet as it should have been. It didn't taste of much at all other than water. Think more like a sorbet but with none of the taste. Most of the Americans seemed to bring sauce to help remedy this situation and were usually polite enough to share once you'd jammed yourself in the seat next to them. I don't know why, but despite bringing all sorts of food along in my luggage, I never once remembered sauce for the ice cream.

On Sunday nights the cafe had a pizza night. They were pretty good as long as you were prepared to wait an unspecific but usually long time for it to turn up.

After about six months, I had a slight change in circumstances. While some of the security team stayed in the hotel (out of preference or otherwise) a number of people shared a house on the estate. This was unusual as all the other houses were allocated to Exxon staff with spouses. Even as hatted contractors, we shouldn't have been afforded the use of a house. It would seem the residents liked having a security team next door though, as one was given over to us. There were four bedrooms and when one person left, I was invited to take their room.

This was quite a game-changer as it meant I had permanent access to a comfy and sociable lounge, dining room and even a kitchen. It was a bit like being a student again, but this time my house mates were tidy and got up before noon.

It also meant I could cook for myself again, which I did at least once a week. I would probably have cooked more than that, but getting groceries was awkward. We had to go to the market trying to find vegetables we recognised while Anietie shouted at the traders for trying to rip us off. To be fair, I didn't care if they charged us the equivalent of 30p instead of 10p for a bag of onions, but for Anietie it seemed to be a point of principle.

Meat was a different matter. We actually passed by a butcher's shop most mornings on the way to work. It was nothing more than a big table by the side of the road. Depending on when we went passed, we'd either see a stressed looking cow on a rope, or a table full of meat. While it was definitely fresh, the hygiene standards were questionable.

A lot of the meat we got came via helicopter from Port Harcourt. It was probably another abuse of company resources but it could have been officially sanctioned to keep us relatively sane. The meat delivery was monthly and we had to place our order in advance. We could order chicken, sausages, burgers and so on, much more than was available locally.

Sometimes we'd organise a BBQ at the house, with one Aussie SAS guy called Stewart doing all the cooking. He claimed that as an Australian, barbecuing was in his blood and we weren't allowed anywhere near the grill.

Stewart once declared that if I wasn't such a good cook (apart from the BBQ, obviously), he would have kicked me out of the house. He was a self-declared 'bloke' that enjoyed beer, football and other butch activities. His nickname was 'Slam' because he'd been punched in the face so many times, apparently due to his enjoyment of a good bar fight. I disliked football and would instead chuck disco music on the stereo given half a chance, possibly even dancing out a few shapes. It was not anything he was used to. I'm mostly sure he was only kidding about throwing me out.

My buddy Barry brought the best meat though. Back in the USA, he spent his spare time hunting deer on a lodge that he co-owned with a bunch of other enthusiasts. Occasionally he'd use a gun but his weapon of choice was a bow. He would get his kills professionally butchered and would occasionally bring some over to Nigeria.

Barry managed this by freezing the meat and then storing it in a taped-up solid cool-box along with generous amounts of dry ice. He'd then just stick it in as baggage at the airport. Amazingly, this was enough to keep the contents frozen on its journey across three continents. Given that it clearly looked like a cool-box, I always expected it to get impounded en-route, but it never happened. Safely hidden in the box would be steaks, brisket and some amazing giant sausages. Barry was very popular when he arrived.

CHAPTER THIRTY-FOUR

Nigerian Life

I've discussed what life was like for me in Nigeria, but what about life for Nigerians? Breakfast and then out for a hard day of scamming? Not really, but often the lines between scamming and normal business are blurred anyway. The term we heard a lot was 'dash', which could be money for a scam but could equally refer to a fairly earned tip.

Despite the dubious morality of scamming, a great proportion of Nigerians seemed to take their faith and religion seriously. The choice of faith was largely defined by a geographical split, with the northern half of the country being predominantly Muslim and the southern half dominated by Christianity. Churches were a common sight and were well attended on Sundays, at least in our part of the world. Women would dress up in the finest outfits, with brightly coloured and gravity-defying head pieces routinely worn. I pity whoever was sitting on the row behind them.

I wish I had taken more photos of the church names as a reminder, they were typically long, flamboyant and very entertaining. It was as if the church's pecking order could be determined by the outlandishness of its title. But who was to say if the 'Fountain of Life Miracle Ministry' was any better than the 'Mount Zion Lighthouse Full Gospel Church Inc' right next door?

Despite their religious convictions, belief in other forces seemed rife including a non-specific sort of local magic. One helpful local offered to use magic to help out Mike, one of our team, with a problem he had with his feet. The man brought forth his mystical 'Ju-Ju' powers to rid Mike of whatever ailment was bothering him. To us, it just looked like someone had taken Mike's trainers and hung them in a tree for a while.

Someone casting magical spells on trainers was pretty funny for us and I'm fairly sure the locals were just trying to entertain us with their antics as well. Neither party seemed to take it very seriously but other aspects of the local beliefs could have more serious consequences. It was quite common to entrust a local witch doctor with any medical matters, despite the availability of more conventional medical care. Dubious cures would be offered for serious conditions, such as malaria which was both debilitating and common.

The worst reminder was the constant presence of the so-called witch children. These poor kids had been cast from their homes on the advice of a witch doctor on the grounds that they had been cursed or were possessed by the devil. It is beyond my understanding how anyone could throw out a family member based on such flimsy and whimsical guidance. A group of these witch children had taken up residence at the end of the road outside our hotel. Their accommodation was little more than a hedge and can't have given them much protection.

Despite feeling sorry for their situation, we were strongly warned against intervening and helping the children. The locals seemed happy to tolerate the witch children in their chosen location, but if we attempted to help them out, we would be ostracised ourselves. Things could get serious very quickly and it wasn't unknown for workers to need to make a sharp exit from the country when a visa was revoked. This was one area where interference in local culture would not be tolerated. Looking back, my small guilt at not helping has grown and I wonder if I could have done more. I have vague memories that we occasionally gave money to Anietie to give to the children, but that could be my memory hoping for the best.

While I lived and worked with Nigerians, I would be lying if I said I lived like a local. I had the privilege of living in a bubble, even if it was a tarnished version of what I was used to. I recognise that most locals would have considered themselves very luckily to enjoy the space I had. Most neighbourhood houses were concrete cubes with a metal roof and open windows. Running water and electricity were limited, with many people making use of small generators to provide power only when they needed it. These were noisy and polluting. Roadside shops were often of similar construction, although many were even simpler and little more than a tarpaulin stretched over a wooden frame. Wares of all kinds would adorn every possible space, dangling precariously.

There were many cars on the road, but by far the most common form of transport was the motorbike. The bikes were cheap models imported from China and were nearly all identical in general style. They were often very overloaded and it was common to see a whole family of four or five riding together, all crammed onto a single long seat. Almost nobody wore a helmet and even when they did, the helmet was frequently something that barely counted, such as an upturned bucket or tub with hole cut in it for the rider to poke their face through. It was very comical to see, but I would also wince inwardly at the safety implications. It was also uncomfortable to watch the rider and their passengers when the rain arrived, soaking them all to the skin.

Fortunately, the high temperatures meant they would dry off pretty quickly as well.

The bikes were used to transport more than just people and would often be carrying the most outlandish loads. Size, manoeuvrability and fragility rarely seemed to be a concern and we often saw bundles of logs carried sideways or crates of glass bottles rattling along at high speed. Sometimes a single passenger was onboard as well, tasked with holding onto whatever was being precariously transported. On our daily commute we would delight at spotting something particularly daft or dangerous, such as a passenger struggling to hold onto a giant sheet of glass against the buffeting wind.

Despite the challenges, I got the impression that most people were generally happy. People smiled, enjoyed life and danced when the music was right.

CHAPTER THIRTY-FIVE

Customs inspection, duck!

One of the odd quirks I learnt about ex-military types is their love for their own memorabilia. Medals, plaques and team photos are all part of the norm in any military outfit in the world. Clearly this was something they felt they were missing out on and decided it would be a good idea if the security team had its own insignia. Amusingly, the guy that organised all this was Dave, the only other person in our team without a military background. He was a former policeman and had the unenviable job of investigating possible fraud cases. Naturally Dave had plenty to do.

As 'the IT guy', I was drafted in to help make this suggestion into a reality. Because obviously when there's a fully-fledged IT expert available, everyone else forgets how to drive a mouse.

Rather than create the whole thing from scratch, I started off with an existing insignia and then doctored it heavily to meet our own needs. I went through a few designs until the final version was universally approved.

As we were in house number 37, we became 37 Squadron. This was a double whammy as the much-enjoyed local rum was called Squadron Rum. The centre of the badge sported a mosquito and below that was written Night Fighter. This was less to show our support of the local working ladies and more a humorous way to have hooker written on the badge in a way that wouldn't be obvious to most people. Finally, at the bottom was written 'Wise without eyes', taken from the motto of a genuine British RAF squadron, also with the number 37, that had flown in the second world war.

Clearly it was a patchwork of influences but the final result was quite convincing as an actual insignia. We referred to ourselves as 37 Squadron on occasion and somebody even went as far as to have caps and polo shirts made up. The caps were terrible, the stitching was so poor as to make the design unreadable. The polo shirts turned out very well though and I still have mine in a drawer somewhere. As well as the insignia on the left breast, the logo for Squadron Rum was stitched onto the right arm, making it appear as if we had official sponsorship.

It wasn't the only thing I took home. A few local shops sold art to the oil workers. That must have been it because there weren't many tourists passing through. I bought a simple painting of a village scene which I framed and hung some years later. I also bought a tribal mask, made of wood and painted plain black.

While these were clearly recent creations, you had to be careful not to be stung for 'antiquities tax' when trying to leave the country. This was a blatant attempt to screw you for money, but it could still be successful unless you were willing to abandon your purchases at the airport.

In the absence of proper airport scanners, all bags were visually inspected before being passed over for loading on the aircraft. It wasn't exactly a fun process.

My wife (then girlfriend) had given me a rubber duck from a trip she'd made to Berlin. The duck was a bit unusual in that it was black with a yellow beak rather than the other way around.

The first time I left the country, my duck was perched on the top of all my stuff in my bag. It wasn't planned, but when the guard when into my bag for a rummage around, he was totally distracted by the duck. He picked it up, chuckled, showed his colleague before returning the duck (Bernie) to my bag. That was the end of the inspection.

Thereafter, every time I went through the inspection, I made sure Bernie was at the top. He never let me down and I escaped paying any nonsense scam tax on my goodies.

Getting home was usually a delight. After so many weeks, it was great to head home for a break and some normality. For the few days before heading home you were declared 'demob happy' and nothing could dampen your mood.

This was true for me for all but one flight back. A few days before my planned return for Christmas, the airport in Lagos declared that the runway was out of action.

They only had two runways, one for local short-haul flights and a longer runway for the bigger aircraft going on longer journeys. The constant hammering of daily flights from the heavier aircraft had caused jarring and dangerous potholes. And these ones couldn't be filled with sand.

For all the time I'd been going in and out, we'd been using the short runway. This led to some interesting take-offs and landings, as we would either accelerate or decelerate quite harshly due to the much shorter length. The increase in traffic plus the abuse from the heavier aircraft quickly shredded the shorter runway too, so much so that it too was unusable.

For several nail-biting days I waited to hear if either runway could be repaired enough for my flight to continue. It was, but with one drawback. To help matters, the airline chose to take off with almost no fuel. This made us lighter, faster and in the event of a crash, meant we wouldn't turn into a giant fireball. This was great to start with, but with the obvious problem that once up in the air, we still didn't have any fuel.

We flew a relatively short distance over two other countries to reach Accra in Ghana where we refuelled. Ghana was apparently blessed with a whole runway without too many holes. From there we could complete our journey back to the UK without further incident. What a relief!

CHAPTER THIRTY-SIX

Lockdowns and golf

I still didn't have a great deal to do at work, but life was becoming generally easier and the various social events I routinely attended helped a great deal. Living in the house was also far preferable to the loneliness of the hotel room.

But as with lots of things in life, just when you think you've nailed it, the rules change.

The security situation since I'd arrived in Nigeria had been pretty relaxed. There were occasional kidnappings, but these were financially motivated and so, unlike Iraq, you were likely to return with your head still on your shoulders.

The situation was worse a couple of hundred miles or so further west, where greater political motivation had led to some kidnappings turning ugly. Nigeria is very tribal though, and as this trouble was in a different tribal area, it might as well have been in a different country.

That's not to say that kidnappings weren't a real risk, it's just that the type of kidnappings that might happen to us couldn't be called kidnappings. At least not to the kidnappers.

If a local leader decided he had an issue with MPN or Exxon, he would like to discuss it with someone. Some of his lads would then go and hunt down someone to attend a meeting, forcibly if necessary. The fact that whoever they caught would almost certainly have no idea about the leader's problem was irrelevant. You were there as a representative of the company and would remain there until the issue was resolved.

The instruction was therefore to phone back and explain that you were in a 'meeting' and that you needed some assistance in sorting things out. If you dared to say that you had been kidnapped, this could immediately sour relations with your host, so you had to go along with the false idea that you were merely in a meeting. Against your will, obviously.

Stewart was unlucky enough to be taken to such a meeting on his first day at the port, which must have been an interesting experience.

The way they took you wasn't at gun point or anything as aggressive as that. A bunch of lads would wait until you were getting in your car and then pile in with you. You'd be crammed into the back seat with more people than seatbelts for a shortish drive to your meeting. The driver would usually go along with it although I'm confident Anietie would have sent them packing.

The problem for the driver was one of loyalty; to their employer or to their local tribe. The employer usually lost, although that wasn't always the case. You really were at the mercy of your driver so it really helped to have a good one who was on your side.

This almost happened to me once. Barry and I were walking through the car park by the badging office on our way back to the main gate. A crowd of lads formed behind us and they were a little clumsy with their intentions. We guessed fairly quickly what they were up to and Barry leaned over to me and laughed.

"What do you think they'll do when they realise we don't have a car?"

As we reached the far side of the car park, they gave up on any pretence that they were just out for a stroll and instead shouted,

"Where is your car?"

We were actually returning on foot all the way, an almost unique habit amongst the foreign workers who largely preferred the safety of travelling by car. On this occasion, not having a car saved us from a mild kidnapping.

As time crept on, things started to get a bit worse. The barrier of tribal separation we'd enjoyed seemed to be weakening, and news of increasingly nearby kidnappings continued to reach us, as did the level of violence that accompanied them.

Any activity with the potential for increased exposure became limited or simply cancelled. This included our river trips and the hash runs. Going running on foot through the jungle on a path that had been marked an hour or two before was clearly always going to be a problem. It felt like all fun had been cancelled, which was rather frustrating.

Things then took a more dramatic turn for the worse. As always, these things start with an ordinary day. We were in the office at the Terminal when word spread of a protest outside. I can't remember what the protest was about, but increasing numbers of people had gathered outside the gate. They'd built speed bumps out of sand that became so big that they were no longer passable.

Despite this, the mood outside and in was still relatively relaxed and a team had been dispatched to negotiate with the crowd. We were instructed to remain onsite and within the perimeter, which we would probably have done anyway.

It's worth explaining at this point how the Terminal was guarded. Drum were employed as part of the security team, but only in an advisory role. We couldn't and wouldn't get involved in the actual physical protection required.

As part of the arrangement with Exxon, the Nigerian government committed to provide a dedicated guard force. I use the word 'dedicated' to describe the organisational structure only; in no way should it be used to infer any sort of commitment by the guard force to their duties.

The guards were known as the Spy Police, which sounds far more exciting than it was. Spy was short for supernumerary, which roughly translated to extra or additional police. In reality they were recruits that had failed to make the grade with the police force and had instead accepted a second-tier role. The Spy Police were almost entirely useless, typically sleeping on the job or accepting bribes to let people past their guard post. And yet they were relied upon to protect both the Terminal and the residence areas.

The only vehicles (and occupants) given any sort of real inspection in and out of the Terminal were those that were part of the security team. For us they tried to do a slightly better job, as if to demonstrate they were useful.

Some of the Spy Police were armed, but I was reliably informed that none of them actually had any bullets. On the rare occasion bullets were issued, they were either sold or shot into the jungle for fun. When the protest was taking place outside the Terminal, the Spy Police simply watched the proceedings and did nothing.

By coincidence, some Nigerian Navy personnel were docked nearby and trying to go along the road that was blocked. They were armed with guns and ammunition but not diplomacy skills. When they failed to gain safe passage through the blockade, they drew their weapons and fired into the crowd, injuring several protesters and killing at least one.

What had started out as a lively, if inconvenient, protest had escalated very rapidly into a very serious situation. Instead of dispersing the crowd, the numbers began to increase further. Things started happening quickly then and a small number of protesters attempted to kidnap a chap who happened to be just outside the gates. It was unplanned as they didn't have a car to transport their victim. Instead, they bundled him onto the back of a motorbike and drove off. While there were enough individuals to compel him to get on the bike to begin with, that wasn't the case as soon as they got moving.

As the bike then slowed again, he took the initiative and leapt off and away from his would-be kidnappers. Running, he made for a guardhouse manned by the Spy Police and hid in one of the rooms inside. To his horror, instead of protecting him as he'd hoped, the guards let the kidnappers in and even pointed out where he was trying to hide.

At first the kidnappers tried to drag him out, but when that proved difficult, they threatened him with a machete. Unsure what to do next, he protected his head and balled up on the floor. Then they began swinging the machete at him.

Thankfully they used the flat side instead of the blade. After a couple of body blows, they gave up and left him sore, bruised but alive on the floor. Understandably, he was very shaken up and managed from there to make it safely back inside the boundary of the Terminal.

As soon as news of that attack reached the security team, the entire Terminal went into full lockdown. As well as closing all the gates, we were further confined to our offices. For the first time in my tenure, the emergency control room in our building burst into life and I was in the odd situation of having all the senior staff from the Terminal sharing my normally quiet building. They even took advantage of some of my biscuits.

Thankfully things began to cool off a bit although there remained a sort of stalemate. Guards patrolled the fence line inside while groups of men roamed outside armed with rudimentary weapons like short metal poles or chains. We watched them as closely as we dared through binoculars.

The Nigerian Army were called in to bolster our incompetent guards at the main entrances, including what looked like an armoured personnel carrier at the main gate. The evening wore on without further incident and it looked like we would have to spend the night in our offices. We started trying to line up chairs to make makeshift beds.

Then at around 1am, we got the message that the crowd outside had dispersed, the speed bumps had been flattened and we were going to be escorted back to Eket and the relative safety of the housing estate. It was an odd journey back that night. I'd never done it in the dark before. Under the glare of our headlights and after the events of the day, even the outline of the jungle seemed more hostile. There was a long convoy back with military vehicles interspersed between our regular cars.

Nothing happened on the way back, but it was a long night in house 37 as the team tried to ensure everyone was safe and accounted for.

The next day I attended a meeting with a large group of very worried people. No one had gone back to the Terminal that morning and we remained in the housing compound. The meeting took place in the largest room they could find in the hotel and a senior representative from Exxon, called Dick, attempted to answer questions.

Reassurances that we were ably protected by the Spy Police at the gates weren't well received. Someone asked about the attempted kidnapping and whether the man involved was ok. Dick began by saying he thought the man was okay and not really that badly hurt. That was fine until a voice piped up from the back, "No I'm not!". He wasn't fine but he was very pissed off! The entire story was then relayed first-hand to the audience. This helped to fill in the gaps but probably didn't do much for the confidence in our guard force.

The Terminal remained out-of-bounds for everyone except a skeleton crew running essential systems and a few of the security team. Those like me that didn't need to be there were confined to the housing estate and that continued to be the situation for a full three weeks. During this time the Exxon team negotiated with the locals, presumably paying out a sum of money to the families of the deceased and injured, despite the fact that they hadn't actually been responsible.

As in Iraq, you can't be scared all the time, and the fearful excitement of the protest descended into the boredom of lockdown. We tried to find entertainment to keep us occupied, including playing golf across the front lawns around the housing estate.

The pool and cafe became more of a focal point and we even managed one or two lockdown parties. We settled into a new routine, one with even less to do than usual. About the time the lockdown finished, my stint finished and I flew home. In the four or so weeks I'd been in Nigeria, I'd spent three weeks of it in the confines of the small housing estate.

CHAPTER THIRTY-SEVEN

A declining situation

On my return to Africa, things had opened up again, but the situation was still pretty dire. Although there were no more significant events, the threat remained. Once or twice lockdown was re-established, just as a precautionary measure.

Inevitably, this made people a bit jumpy and the Blitz spirit that had existed during our first lockdown started to diminish. Increasingly people just sat around in their houses and rooms to wait it out. We didn't even play golf again.

By this time, I was approaching my one-year anniversary with Drum Cussac and the minimum I'd committed to Jeremy that I would do. After some soul-searching, and considering a few options, I decided I'd had enough of Nigeria.

Ignoring all the varying frustrations of daily life, it wasn't really giving me any career development. The challenges you face in your job ought to be more around learning new skills than dealing with boredom and potential kidnapping. My role had very much subsided into the category of 'character building', if we were going to be generous.

With regards to my actual work, the building work wasn't

a great deal further along and the installers were still 'about two weeks' away from returning. It didn't appear as if I'd be doing anything fruitful anytime soon.

I contacted Jeremy and explained my intention to leave and he was very understanding. I'd failed to outlast Ken, but I'd managed better than a lot of others before me. I left Nigeria one year and one day after I had first arrived.

My timing was pretty good. A few months after I left, a group of locals stormed into Nancy's, although not on fish and chip night. They shot and killed the solitary guard on the gate before rounding up a group that had been sitting in the bar. The group were taken by road a short distance and then transferred to a boat where they vanished up-river and into the jungle.

Exxon received ransom demands for the return of their employees and to start with at least, tried to play hard ball.

One poor lady received a phone call from a member of the kidnapped group to say that her husband had been shot. It was actually only a ruse to increase pressure and obtain the ransom payout. It worked and Exxon duly coughed up. The husband was returned safe and well, along with the others but it must have been a horrendous experience for all involved.

Looking back now after many years have passed, it's hard to decide whether going out to Nigeria was a good idea or not. I didn't learn much in the way of new technical skills, but in fairness, losing a year in my career path has had no noticeable impact. On the flip side, it probably did teach me a great deal about my own limits and about a people and culture very different to my own. I also built on my ability to remain relatively cool under pressure and the importance of maintaining a sense of humour when things are crumbling around you. With the benefit of hindsight, I am definitely glad to have spent that time in Iraq and the Middle East. And

I would *probably* choose to go back to Nigeria.

If I had the opportunity now to return to either country, I would definitely go back. But perhaps for no more than a fortnight in that particular African country. With some snacks, obviously.

Despite all the challenges, I have enjoyed all my travels and continued to do so after the adventures that I've written about here. Although for later journeys I stuck to countries that didn't feature in the top ten of the world's most dangerous (at the time of my travels, I think Iraq was seventh and Nigeria was eighth).

CHAPTER THIRTY-EIGHT

Epilogue

I hope you have enjoyed reading about my misadventures. I've enjoyed writing about them more than I'd expected and it's probably been quite cathartic.

It would be hard to recommend my path to others. Extreme backpacking in war zones with your own protection team isn't an option available to most. I have been privileged enough to live and work alongside some incredibly skilled, talented and dedicated individuals. I was well looked after, protected and ultimately survived all that was thrown at me. I can take credit for some of this but I am also thankful for the kindness and support of others. And I made some good friends along the way.

To those that I've left out but deserved a mention, I wholeheartedly apologise. And also to those I included but misrepresented or short-changed.

And finally thank you to you, my reader, for coming along on this journey of self-indulgence and proving that someone other than me thinks my tales might be interesting. You've made it to the end.

Thank you! Graeme Simpson